Contents

8 Working with tables   **97**

9 Working with pictures   **111**

10 Considering page design   **123**

Introducing Publisher

Welcome to *Publisher 2000 in easy steps*. This chapter provides a brief introduction to Publisher and the options available to you when you start the program. We also introduce Publisher's star prize – the PageWizards. You can then try out some essentials, like navigating through a document, and learn how to tap the power of the right mouse button.

To provide the greatest possible amount of useful information, hints and tips about working with Publisher, we have assumed that you're familiar with the basics of Microsoft Windows. Enjoy!

Covers

Chapter One

Starting Publisher

To start Publisher, first click the Start button on the Windows Task bar. Then, move the mouse pointer up the menu options and click on Programs, followed by Microsoft Publisher as illustrated below:

You can start Publisher with fewer actions by creating a Windows shortcut and placing it on the Desktop. See your Windows user guide for instructions.

In the Help menu, Publisher provides the Detect and Repair command to help check and repair non-essential files like fonts and templates.

Publisher now provides lots of options for users with disabilities: type 'accessibility' in the online Help system to find out more.

Desktop shortcut

2 Then click here.

3 Finally, click here to start Publisher.

| Click here.

Windows Desktop

Windows Task bar

By default, as soon as you click on Publisher 2000 in step 3 above, Publisher displays the Catalog – from where you can choose one of the three options shown on the opposite page:

...cont'd

Those who use Microsoft Office will find Publisher is now even easier to learn: it follows the Microsoft Office way of doing things.

To quickly choose a design or style, simply double-click the desired PageWizard icon.

If you create your own document templates, you can easily gain access to them later by clicking the Templates button.

If more designs are available than Publisher can currently display, you can use the scroll buttons to bring the remaining options into view.

- You can tell Publisher to create a new publication based on one of the many cleverly designed interactive templates already predesigned for you. This involves using a PageWizard, which asks you some simple questions, and then creates the basic layout for you

- Or if you're feeling creative, you can choose the Blank Publications tab, then choose an option from a series of page sizes and types – and perform the entire page design yourself

- Or you can open an existing Publisher document

Click here to see the range of PageWizards available

Click here to see the Wizard-driven templates organised into design sets

Click here to see the range of 'blank page' options available

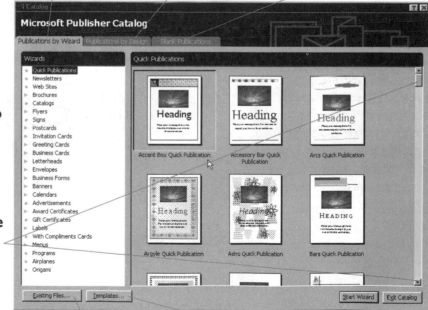

Click here to display a list of existing Publisher documents

Click here to view any templates that you've made

Introducing the PageWizards

We'll look at opening existing publications and creating your own publications from the beginning later in this book. For now, let's take a brief look at PageWizards.

If you choose a PageWizard, Publisher does most of the hard work of designing the layout of your publication for you, while still giving you a lot of control over how your publication will eventually look. You simply make your choices at each stage, and you can even go back to previous stages to try out other designs. And remember, even if you've already chosen a PageWizard design, you can still edit the design to suit your needs whenever you wish.

So let's imagine you've chosen the Newsletters PageWizard. The following dialog box presents you with a range of Web page designs. Let's examine these below:

Each time you move your selection, Publisher usually updates the preview image so at each stage you can immediately see how your publication structure is developing. If you're not happy with the results, simply choose an alternative design element from the Wizard component list displayed on the left-most part of your screen.

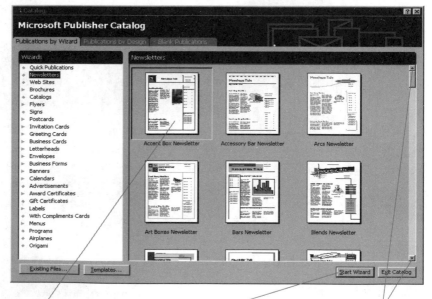

2 Click to select the design you want.

3 Click here to start the design Wizard and make further choices.

| Click these if you want to see further designs (if available).

The Publisher screen

 To quickly learn more about a tool on a toolbar, position the mouse pointer directly on top of the desired tool. Publisher then names the tool (ScreenTip) and briefly describes its purpose.

 The unlabelled elements on the screen are common components of Windows programs. See your Windows documentation for more information.

 The toolbars, rulers and status bar can be turned on or off by clicking the right mouse button on the non-printing workspace area and choosing the desired option from the menu.

When you start Publisher and choose a PageWizard from the Catalog, or the Blank Publication option, Publisher clears away the Catalog dialog box to reveal the Publisher screen. This is where you can create, edit, view, manipulate and save your publication.

Objects toolbar   Rulers   Menu bar   Standard toolbar   Formatting toolbar   Title bar

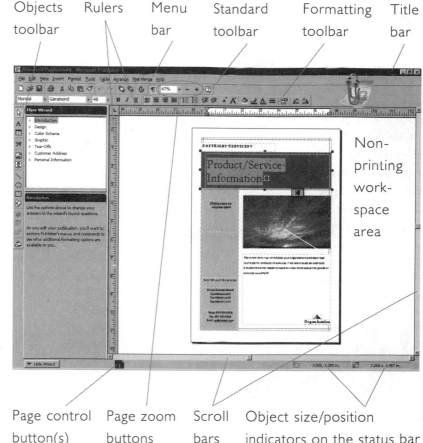

Non-printing work-space area

Page control button(s)   Page zoom buttons   Scroll bars   Object size/position indicators on the status bar

The toolbars

The Standard, Formatting and Objects toolbars contain buttons to provide quick access to commands. You click a button to gain access to the desired command. When you click on some buttons, Publisher may display other tools or toolbars to extend or customize your choices further.

Selecting

With the Pointer (selection) tool active, you can select several objects at once. Drag a rectangular selection box around the objects you want to select.

If you have several objects on the screen, you can keep precise control of which objects you select, by pressing and holding down the SHIFT key as you click objects in sequence.

Sometimes, the desired object may be behind another larger object, making it difficult to select. If this happens, select the largest object (nearest to you), then choose the Send Backward or the Send to Back commands on the Arrange menu.

In Publisher, you select something if you want to affect the selected item in a particular way. For example, to change the size and proportions of a drawn rectangle, you must select the rectangle first. Only then can you change the height, width, or both, or modify the rectangle.

When you click an object, you select it. Publisher then places selection handles around the selected object:

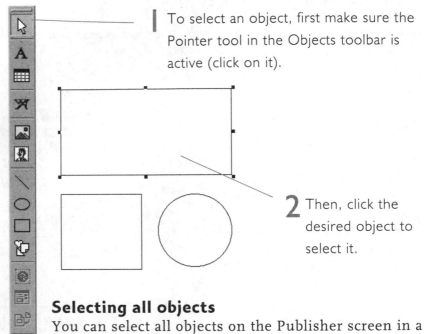

1 To select an object, first make sure the Pointer tool in the Objects toolbar is active (click on it).

2 Then, click the desired object to select it.

Selecting all objects

You can select all objects on the Publisher screen in a single action by clicking Select All in the Edit menu. To clear the selection, click anywhere outside of the selection.

If you can't select an object

If the object you want to select does not appear to be selectable, the object may have been placed on the background. We'll discuss the background in detail in Chapter 2; for now, a quick way to move to the background is to press the CTRL+M keys. This is a shortcut way of choosing the Go to Background command in the View menu. Press CTRL+M again to return to 'normal' view.

Moving around a publication

If your publication is made up of more than a single page, and you're seeing your pages in Single page view, you can choose to view adjacent pages side by side, by opening the View menu and choosing the Two-Page Spread command.

If you select an object before you zoom in or out, any following zoom action is centred on the selected object, rather than the entire page.

To quickly switch between the current zoom value and actual page size, press the F9 key. Each time you press F9, the current view toggles.

Publisher provides several tools to enable you to move around a publication.

The scroll bars

Click the horizontal or vertical scroll buttons on the horizontal and vertical scroll bars to scroll the publication page up or down, and left or right.

To move quickly, drag the scroll box along the bar, or click a location on the bar representing where you want to go

The page control buttons

To move to a desired page, you can use the page control buttons situated at the lower-most left-hand corner of the Publisher window. See the illustration below:

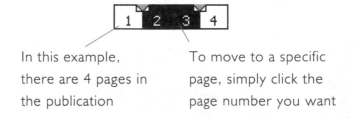

In this example, there are 4 pages in the publication

To move to a specific page, simply click the page number you want

The page zoom controls

You can easily move your publication page or selected object closer or further away using the page zoom controls situated on the Standard toolbar (see page 11).

Click here to display the Zoom options menu

Click here to zoom out

Click here to zoom in

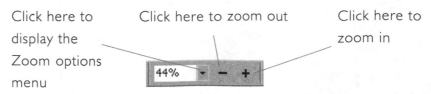

Tracking objects on the workspace

Situated towards the lower right of the Publisher window, the object size and position indicators provide you with the continual feedback that is necessary to place objects accurately on your publication pages.

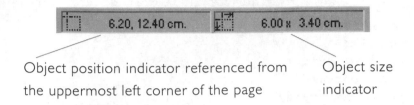

Object position indicator referenced from the uppermost left corner of the page

Object size indicator

If you can't see the object size and position indicators, the Status bar may have been hidden to create more space on the screen. To re-display the Status bar, open the View menu, then click the Toolbars command followed by Status Bar.

When no object is selected, the object position indicator tracks the mouse pointer. You can change the measurement units used easily, as shown below.

Changing the measurement units

Click the Options command in the Tools menu to display the Options dialog box. Then, in the Options dialog box, you can specify whether to use inches, centimetres, picas or points, as shown in the screen shot below.

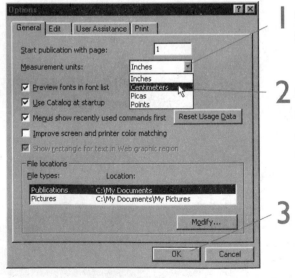

l Click here to open the drop-down list.

2 Click on a new measurement choice from the list.

3 Click here to confirm your new choice.

Using Undo and Redo

Instead of using the toolbar Undo/ Redo buttons, you can use the Undo command in the Edit menu. Undo can reverse up to 20 of the most recent actions. The Edit menu commands are sometimes better in that they provide precise information about the type of object that the Undo action is affecting.

Publisher provides two commands which are so important that some mention of them should be included early on in this book. Undo reverses the most recent editing action or command you chose. Redo simply reverses your most recent Undo.

For example, let's assume you've inserted a piece of clip art into your publication and resized the picture, but then you realise the picture size is still 'wrong'. At this stage, you have several options. You can, of course, simply resize it again to the desired size. Alternatively – and arguably this is the safest course – you can simply click on the Undo button situated on the Standard toolbar.

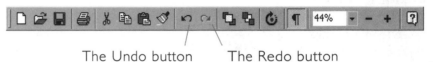

The Undo button   The Redo button

If Undo is available, remember, for Undo to work, you must choose Undo before pressing any key or clicking a mouse button elsewhere.

An important fact to note is that Undo only reverses the most recent command or editing action. So, to continue our previous example, if you had realised that your original resized picture was still the wrong size, but went on to perform some other keyboard operation or mouse click before choosing Undo, then Undo would not restore the original picture size. Therefore, the three golden rules to remember when using Undo are:

1. If you realise that you've made a mistake, immediately pause.

2. Certainly consider your next action but remember: don't press any keys or click the mouse.

3. Then, choose Undo *immediately*.

Some commands and editing actions cannot be undone.

Using Redo

To reverse the most recent Undo, you simple choose the Undo command again – except this time, it's called Redo. If you were to choose the command again, the action would once again change back to Undo, and so on.

The right mouse button shortcuts

If you click the right mouse button while the mouse pointer is placed over several selected objects, the command you choose applies to all the selected objects. For example, using this method, you can delete multiple objects quickly.

In Publisher, the right mouse button can be used extensively to provide powerful shortcuts to some of the more commonly used commands and procedures.

The specific commands that appear on the floating menus when you click the right mouse button depend on the location of the mouse pointer at the time you click, and on which, if any, objects are selected. For example, if you click the right mouse button while the mouse pointer is on a free space area, Publisher displays a floating menu which includes commands that relate to the display of toolbars, rulers and the Status bar. Other commands are made available when you click the right mouse button over selected objects. Some examples are shown below.

The Office Assistant can be turned on or off: by default, Publisher makes it available to help you at all times.

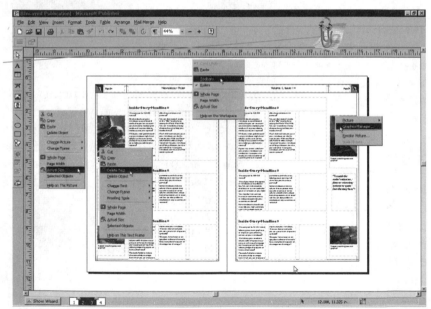

Click the right mouse button to display a floating menu. You can then click either mouse button to choose a command from the menu.

Applying formatting quickly

With the right mouse button, drag an object or text whose formatting you want to copy, onto the object or text where you want to apply the formatting. Release the right mouse button and Publisher displays a floating menu. Choose the Apply Formatting Here command to copy the formatting.

Getting started with the basics

In this chapter, we examine how to start, open and close a publication in Publisher, and how to set up a new publication for commercial printing. We also explore some of the different ways in which you can insert and manipulate information within documents.

Covers

Chapter Two

Starting a new publication

The **Quick Publication Wizard is new to Publisher 2000 (see the screenshot on page 9 for how to access this); it helps you to quickly and easily design and layout a 1-page publication.**

After starting Publisher, arguably the quickest way to create a publication might be to use a PageWizard as discussed in the previous chapter. However, if you want to start a new publication based entirely on your own design and creativity, in the Catalog dialog box, click on the Blank Publications tab to see a range of publication templates.

As you can see below, Publisher provides several blank page options by presetting the margins and page size for the type of blank page publication you choose:

If you **don't see the desired template, click here to access the Page Setup options. You can then confirm your choices directly in the Page Setup dialog box.**

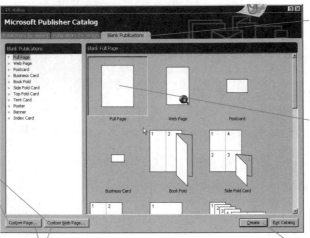

1 Click here to list the Blank page templates.

2 To select a template, click the desired template picture.

3 If you want to specify your own page size and setting, click the desired Custom button and make your choices in the Page Setup dialog box.

4 Click here to confirm your choice of template.

To tell **Publisher not to display the Catalog dialog box each time you start Publisher, choose Options from the Tools menu. Next, clear the Use Catalog At Startup check box, then click OK.**

Establishing your target printer

After you've decided the type of publication you want to create, next you must tell Publisher the name of the printer to which you intend to print your final publication. The choice of printer affects the size of the printable area on your page, the page sizes available, margin widths, fonts available to your publication, and so on. Therefore, this must be done soon after you start your publication.

Once you've chosen a publication template, if you change your mind, you can still display the Catalog dialog box at any time by choosing the New command in the File menu.

 If, after laying out your publication, you change your target printer, when you print your publication it may not look as you intended: fonts may be missing or substituted, and page sizes and margins may differ.

 If you're going to use external word-processed files and clip art in your publication, now is a good time to make sure you have these ready and available for Publisher to use.

You can set your target printer by first opening the File menu and clicking the Print Setup command to display the Print Setup dialog box. Then perform the following steps:

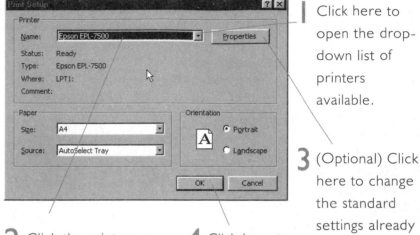

1 Click here to open the drop-down list of printers available.

3 (Optional) Click here to change the standard settings already established for your desired printer.

2 Click the printer you want to use as your target printer (if you're using an outside printer, see overleaf.

4 Click here to confirm your options.

Using an outside print shop

If you plan to use a commercial print shop to print your final publication, you'll need to establish the setup now before adding design components to your pages. This aspect is covered in depth overleaf.

Many print organizations now accept Publisher files, without any conversion needed by you. This can obviously ensure your publishing task is easier and can indeed save you money. Key point: find a reliable print shop that can demonstrate a track record of working with Publisher files. Ideally, get personal recommendations from friends, colleagues or business contacts before making your choice.

Preparing for commercial printing

Once you've decided on the type of publication you want, if you're going to use an outside printing service to print your final publication, you need to establish your printing options now – *before* adding the design components to your page!

Establishing which type of commercial printing to use

You have three printing choices:

- Black and white

- Process-colour

- Spot-colour

The benefits and drawbacks of these printing processes are described in more detail on pages 167–169.

To set up your document for the type of printing you want, first open the Tools menu and choose the Commercial Printing Tools command followed by the Color Printing command. Then perform the following steps:

For black and white printing:

 Publisher provides some excellent advice and information about using outside print services. Type Outside Printing Services into your Publisher online Help to learn more.

 **You can find out more about using a commercial print shop on pages 167–169.**

1 Click the Spot Color(s) option button.

2 Click Change Spot Color.

3 Click Black And White only.

4 Click OK twice.

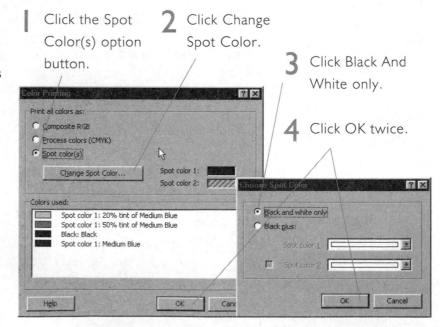

...cont'd

For process-colour printing:

1 Click the Process Color(s) (CMYK) option button.

When your publication is ready, make sure you use the Pack and Go command on the File menu to ensure your printer receives all the necessary files to complete your print job.

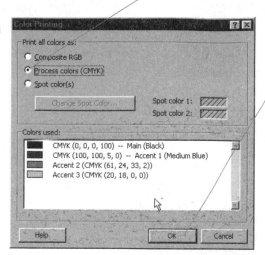

2 Click the OK button. Publisher then establishes (or changes any existing objects to) CMYK values and creates the four colour plates: C (Cyan), M (Magenta), Y (Yellow), and K (stands for blacK).

If you change your mind and decide you want to print to your desktop printer instead, in the Color Printing dialog box, under the 'Print all colors as:' category, simply choose the Composite RGB option.

For spot-colour printing:

1 Click the Spot color(s) option button.

2 Click the Change Spot Color option button.

3 Choose the colour(s) you want here.

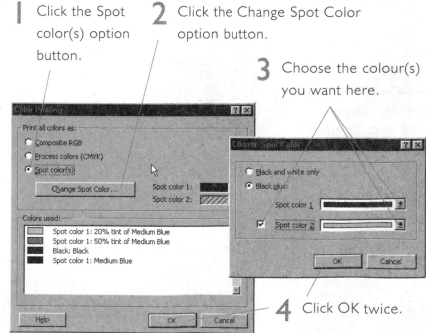

4 Click OK twice.

Opening a publication

In Publisher, you can have only one publication open at any one time. If you try to open a second publication while an existing one is already open, Publisher closes the existing publication before opening the second one.

However, if you want to work on more than one publication at the same time, with one publication already open, you can start Publisher again and open another document, in another Publisher session. Then, in Windows, you can align both Publisher Windows side by side and continue working (see your Windows documentation for more details if required). To open an existing publication, choose the Open command in the File menu. Then perform the following steps:

 To quickly display the Open Publication dialog box using the keyboard, press CTRL+O.

 To quickly display the Open Publication dialog box, click the Open button 📂 on the Standard toolbar.

 Publisher keeps track of the four most recently opened Publisher files and stores their names at the bottom of the File menu. To quickly open any one of these files, click the desired file name.

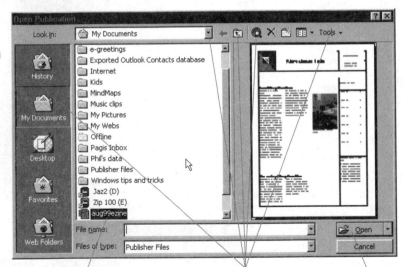

1 Click to select the publication you want.

2 If you can't see the file you want, use the buttons to navigate to its location.

3 Click here.

Opening a Publisher document from the Catalog

If the Catalog dialog box is displayed, you can also click the Existing Files tab to find a desired publication. In the left side pane window, click the publication you want and finally, click the Open button.

Using Publication Design Sets

From Chapter 1, we can see that when you start Publisher, by default, Publisher automatically displays the Catalog – a collection of publication designs. Remember, you can open an existing Publisher document, create an entirely new one using your own settings, or use a PageWizard to help make some important choices for you.

Once you start a Wizard, Publisher takes you step-by-step through the process, and provides plenty of information about your progress based on the choices you make.

If you decide to create a new publication using a Wizard, you can make your choices based on publication type – like newsletter or brochure – or if you want your publication to match other types of publications, you can create a publication based on specific design elements by choosing the Publications by Design tab in the Catalog dialog box. In this way you can ensure your newsletter, for example, uses a design style and colour scheme that matches your stationery, brochures and business cards, and so on:

1 From the File drop-down menu, choose the New command.

2 Click the Publications by Design tab.

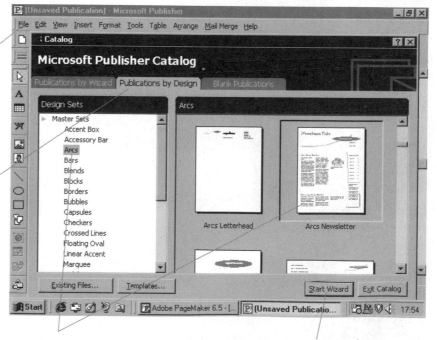

3 Choose your desired design set and particular design.

4 Click here to start the Wizard.

Any changes you've made to the Design Gallery are also recorded when you save.

 Once a Category has been created, you can rename, edit or delete it by first performing steps 1–2 opposite. Then highlight the desired Category, click Options, followed by Edit Categories and choose the Rename command.

 To rename an object, first perform steps 1–2 above. Next, highlight the desired Category and click the right mouse button over the object you want. Then choose the Rename This Object command and complete the sequence.

To add a new design Category to the current publication's Design Set:

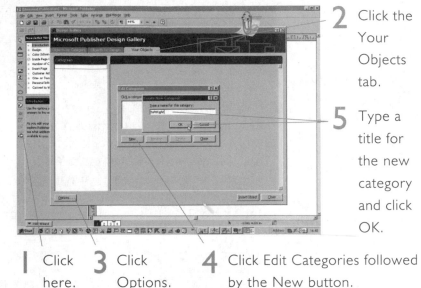

2 Click the Your Objects tab.

5 Type a title for the new category and click OK.

1 Click here.

3 Click Options.

4 Click Edit Categories followed by the New button.

To add an object to a design Category in the current publication's Design Set:

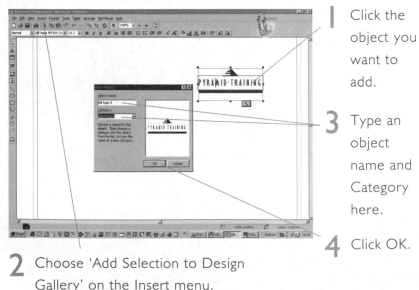

1 Click the object you want to add.

3 Type an object name and Category here.

4 Click OK.

2 Choose 'Add Selection to Design Gallery' on the Insert menu.

A frame for every object

After you've drawn a text frame, you can start entering text immediately – just start typing. If you want to zoom in to the frame, click inside the frame with the right mouse button and choose the Selected Objects command from the floating menu.

WordArt is a program which is available in Publisher if you want to apply some fancy effects to text using different font styles and so on. For example, you can wrap text around a shape, or make a line of text curved like this:

Introducing objects

Until now, we've referred to objects in the general sense. However, in Publisher, the term 'object' has a more precise meaning. An object is simply any independently movable item which you can place and move about on the workspace – for example, a text block, table, or piece of clip art. Objects are examined in more detail in Chapter 3. But for now, we only need to know that most objects in Publisher are placed onto the page using a frame.

Introducing frames

Publisher uses frames to 'hold' objects to make the job of moving objects around easier. Publisher uses different frames to hold the different page design elements of: text, pictures, tables, WordArt (fancy text) and Publisher's own store of pictures, sounds and other objects. Before you can place a design element on a page, you need to create a frame to hold the object. All frames can be resized, moved and aligned precisely using guide lines and ruler marks, and even aligned to other objects on the page.

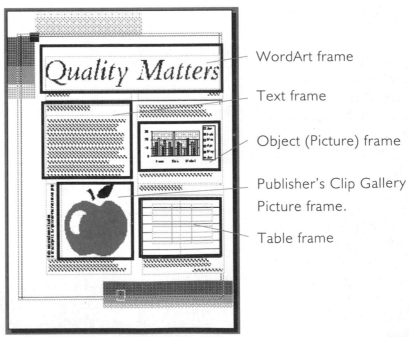

WordArt frame

Text frame

Object (Picture) frame

Publisher's Clip Gallery Picture frame.

Table frame

Creating your frames

The frame tools
To create frames in Publisher, you use the five frame tools situated on the Objects toolbar, as shown below:

To draw the size and position of your frame accurately, watch the mouse pointer indicator on the ruler as you draw your frame. For greater control, you can even drag the horizontal and vertical rulers onto the page if you wish.

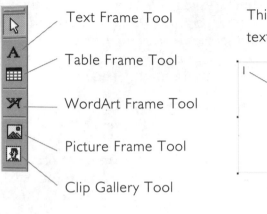

Text Frame Tool

Table Frame Tool

WordArt Frame Tool

Picture Frame Tool

Clip Gallery Tool

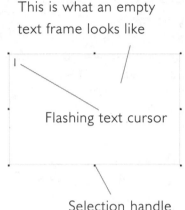

This is what an empty text frame looks like

Flashing text cursor

Selection handle

Creating a frame
To create any frame, perform the following steps:

1 Click a frame tool on the Objects toolbar: the mouse pointer symbol changes to a crosshair shape.

To drag a ruler onto the page, simply place the mouse pointer on to a ruler. The mouse pointer changes to a double arrow symbol. Then drag the desired ruler on to the page. When finished, simply drag the ruler back to its origin.

2 Place the mouse pointer where you want the uppermost left corner of your frame to be situated.

3 Press and hold down the left mouse button while you drag the mouse diagonally down the page to form the lower-most right-hand corner of your frame.

4 When the frame size and shape are correct, release the mouse button: Publisher identifies your frame with a light outline as shown in the illustration above.

Also, after you've drawn a frame, the selected frame has several small black boxes positioned around the frame perimeter: these are the selection handles, which you can use to change the size, shape and position of the frame.

Manipulating frames

You can resize a frame by changing its width, height, or both width and height at the same time. To keep the original frame proportions, press and hold down the SHIFT key while you resize a frame using a corner selection handle. Or, if you want to keep the centre of the frame in the original position, use the CTRL key instead.

To change frame width

1 Hold down the mouse button on the left or right selection handle.

2 Drag the mouse towards the left or towards the right.

 A frame is an object, and as such can be manipulated in various ways. Objects are examined in more detail in Chapter 3.

To change frame height

1 Hold down the mouse button on the top-middle, or bottom-middle selection handle.

2 Drag the mouse upwards or downwards only until you see the desired height.

To change both height and width at the same time

1 Hold down the mouse button on any corner selection handle.

2 Drag diagonally until you see the desired size.

To move a frame

1 Hold down the mouse button anywhere on the perimeter but not on a selection handle.

2 Drag to the new location.

To delete an empty frame

1 Click inside the frame you want to delete.

2 Press the DELETE key.

Flowing text into frames

You can bring text into Publisher in the following ways:

 Once text has been flowed into multiple frames, you can easily follow the 'flow' from one frame to the next simply by clicking the Go To Next Frame and Go To Previous Frame buttons.

- Type directly into a text frame.

- Copy text from another program or file.

- Import an entire text file from another program.

- Import direct from some versions of Microsoft Word.

- Link or embed text using OLE.

Each of these methods will be discussed as we come to them, but for now let's assume you've drawn a text frame. You can then start typing text directly into the frame:

 Where you have multiple connected text frames, if you want to disconnect a text frame from the others, first click in any connected text frame (other than the last in the sequence), then choose the Disconnect Text Frames button on the Standard toolbar:

You can begin typing straight away, and as you enter a line of text, Publisher automatically starts a new line, and so on.

When the text frame fills, Publisher displays the Text Overflow symbol to show that the text frame is full or contains more text than can be seen

1 The Text Overflow symbol (A⋯) appears when there's more text in the frame than can currently be viewed. To flow the remaining hidden text, first draw another text frame.

2 Click the Connect Text Frames button on the Standard toolbar.

3 The mouse pointer then changes into a pitcher symbol. Click in the text frame where you want to place the excess text from the first text frame.

4 Publisher 'pours' the remaining text into the second frame; it places a Go To Next Frame button at the bottom of the first text frame and a Go To Previous Frame button at the top of this frame. Note: the Go To ... buttons are only visible in the frame containing the text cursor.

plays the Text Overflow symbol to show that the text frame is full or contains more text than can be seen.

This remaining text can easily be placed in another text frame. First, open the Tools menu, then

Flowing text from page to page

The Go To Next Frame button looks like this:

The Go To Previous Frame button looks like this:

There's no limit to the number of connected text frames that you can have in a chain.

If, after inserting 'Continue on Page XX' labels, you change your mind, you can remove these labels simply by clearing the desired check boxes in the Text Frame Properties dialog box referred to in step 3. Then click OK.

On the previous page, we examined how to flow text from frame to frame. However, often the text frame into which you want to pour your text may not be situated on the same page. You may start typing text in a text frame, then continue to another text frame on the same page, and finally pour the remaining text into a frame on another page.

By understanding the operation of the text-flow buttons on the page opposite, you can easily track the flow of text in the chain by clicking the Go To Next Frame buttons and the Go To Previous Frame buttons to move through each connected frame in the chain sequence (see margin for visual reminders).

Also, to help your readers follow the text flow, you can tell Publisher to insert 'Continue on page XX' and 'Continued from page XX' labels. To do this, perform the following:

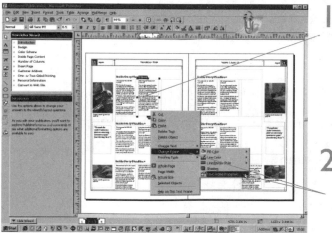

1 With the right mouse button, click a linked text frame.

2 Click Change Frame followed by Text Frame Properties.

3 In the Text Frame Properties dialog box, under the Options category, click one or both 'Include "Continue on Page ..." ' and 'Include "Continued from Page ..." ' check boxes, and click OK.

4 Repeat steps 1 to 3 for each linked frame in the chain on other pages.

The page background

In Publisher, you can place objects that are the same from page to page – like logos and page numbers – on the *background*. All other objects are placed on the *foreground*.

By default, when you're working on a publication, you're actually working on the foreground. So although you can see any objects placed on the background, you cannot directly change, insert or delete background objects.

To work on the background, you must switch to background view. You can then work on the background page in the same way as you do with any other page in Publisher.

To switch to background view, perform the following steps:

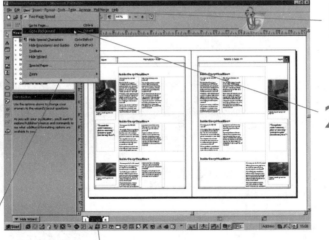

1 Click here to open the View menu.

2 Click here to choose the Go to Background command.

You can quickly establish whether you're viewing the background or the foreground. Simply look at the page buttons situated at the lower left of the screen; if you can see the page numbers, then you're in foreground view. When you're in background view, Publisher does not display page numbers on the page icons. (To return to foreground view, simply select View > Go to Foreground. Alternatively, to toggle between foreground and background view states, press CTRL+M.)

The page background marker

Saving your publication

It's a good idea to save often. With important publications, ideally save at least every 10 minutes.

Once you've established the basic layout of your document, it's a good time to save it. Click the Save button on the Standard toolbar:

or open the File menu, then click Save to display the Save As dialog box:

2 (Optional) choose where you want to store your publication.

You can tell Publisher to prompt you to save at specified intervals. Open the Tools menu and choose Options. Click the User Assistance tab. Next, make sure the 'Remind to save publication' check box contains a tick mark. Then enter the desired value in the associated edit box and click OK.

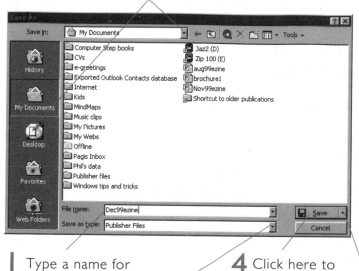

1 Type a name for your publication here.

4 Click here to save (or go to step 5).

3 (Optional) If you use the same style of publication often, you could save it as a template: click here and choose Publisher template.

5 (Optional) To save a backup copy, click here, then choose 'Save with Backup'.

Once you've named a publication, to quickly save it regularly, you can avoid using the menus or toolbar and simply press CTRL+S, if you wish.

After you've saved your publication once, the next time you save, Publisher already knows the filename and so will not display the Save As dialog box again, unless you choose to save your publication to another name, by clicking the Save As command in the File menu.

Closing Publisher

Closing your publication

To close the current Publisher document, open the File menu and click the Close command. If the document you've been working on has not been saved, Publisher displays the following options bubble (or a similar dialog box if you have chosen to hide the Office Assistant):

Before switching off your computer, always save any open files, and close down Publisher (and Windows) using the Exit command, to reduce the possibility of causing damage to your publications.

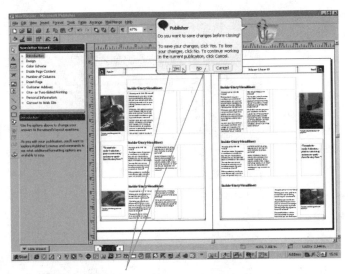

Click Yes to save or click No to close the current publication without saving

To exit Publisher quickly, press ALT+F4. However, if the document has not been saved, Publisher prompts you to save it before exiting.

At this stage, whether you choose to save or not to save, Publisher clears the current publication from the screen and replaces it with a new blank page. You can then start a new publication, open an existing document, or exit Publisher.

Ending a Publisher session

To exit Publisher, click on the Exit command in the File menu. If you have an open publication when you choose the Exit command, Publisher closes the document before exiting the program.

If you've finished your current Publisher session, but still have other programs running, you can provide more memory for the other programs by exiting Publisher.

Working with text and graphic objects

Objects are an important concept in Publisher. In this chapter, we discover commands and techniques that enable you to arrange and manipulate objects, to create some really stunning effects.

Chapter Three

Covers

Using the Format Painter

Remember, you can copy a selected object using the Copy and Paste commands in the Edit menu, or from the pop-up menu when you click the right mouse button on a selected object. However, sometimes you may only want to copy the formatting of an object, not the object itself. Publisher provides a quick and easy way to do this. Select the object whose formatting you want to copy, then carry out the steps below:

You can also use the Format Painter to copy text formatting from one text object to another. First, click in the text frame whose formatting you want to copy. Then perform the steps described on this page.

1 On the Standard toolbar, click the Format Painter button.

There's another way to quickly copy formatting from one object to another. With the right mouse button, drag the object whose formatting you want to copy, onto the target object. Then, from the floating menu, click Apply Formatting Here.

2 As you move the mouse pointer back onto the page, the mouse pointer symbol changes to a Paintbrush.

3 To copy the formatting of the selected object to another single object, click the desired target object. If you want to copy the formatting to several objects, click-and-drag a selection box around the objects to which you want to copy formatting. When you release the mouse pointer, Publisher copies the formatting to the objects you specified.

Moving objects

 You cannot move highlighted text using this technique, as highlighted text is not an object. However, you can use the Cut and Paste commands instead.

 If you want to move a text frame object, position the mouse pointer on the selection perimeter (but not on a selection handle). The Mover symbol will not appear inside a text block object.

 The workspace area surrounding the paper is an ideal place to store objects temporarily.

Moving one or more objects in Publisher is simple. You may want to move objects around the page, from the page to the workspace, and from page to page. To move an object, perform the following steps:

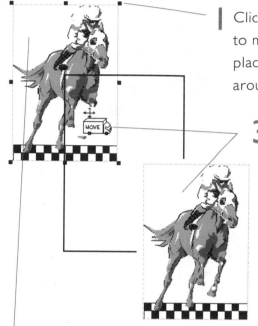

1 Click the object you want to move. Publisher then places selection handles around the object.

3 When the mouse pointer symbol changes to the Mover icon, drag the object to the desired location.

4 Release the left mouse button.

2 Place the mouse pointer over the selected object or on the object's perimeter (but not on a selection handle).

Moving several objects at a time

One way to move several objects together is to hold down SHIFT as you click each object you want to move, and move the mouse pointer over the selection until the Mover symbol appears, then drag to the new location as described above. To constrain the movement to the horizontal or vertical directions only, continue holding down SHIFT until the objects are in the new position and you have released the mouse button.

Resizing objects

To resize using the object centre as the reference point, hold down CTRL while you drag a corner selection handle. But release the mouse button before you release CTRL.

To constrain the resizing action both proportionally and centrally, hold down both SHIFT and CTRL keys as you resize, but release the mouse button before you release SHIFT and CTRL.

When you've selected items to move or resize by dragging, remember, you can also click the right mouse button over the selection to display commands for manipulating objects.

You can easily change the size of any single object or group of objects at any time. When you resize a group of objects, Publisher can temporarily configure the group as a single object. Carry out the following steps to resize objects:

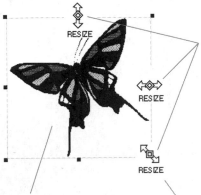

1 Click the object you want to resize. Publisher then places selection handles around the object.

2 Place the mouse pointer over a selection handle, and:
- to change the height, use the middle top or bottom selection handle;
- to change the width, use the middle left or right selection handle;
- to change both height and width at the same time, use a corner selection handle.

3 When the mouse pointer symbol changes to a Resizer symbol, drag to resize the object to the desired size.

To resize a text frame or custom shape keeping to the original proportions, hold down the SHIFT key as you resize, but release the mouse button before you release SHIFT. To resize a picture in the same way, simply perform the action in step 3 above.

Resizing a group of objects

To resize several objects at the same time, hold down SHIFT while you click each object you want to resize. Next, click the Group Objects button at the lower right corner of the selection. Then, perform steps 2 to 3 above and resize as desired. Finally, click the Group Objects button again to ungroup the objects. You can see the Group Objects button in *Grouping and ungrouping objects* on page 41.

Rotating objects

If you change your mind after rotating, click Undo in the Edit menu immediately.

When you position the mouse pointer on a selection handle to rotate an object, if the Rotate symbol does not appear, make sure that you held down ALT before placing the mouse pointer on the handle.

You can also apply these rotation techniques to text in a text frame.

To constrain the rotation action to 15 degree intervals, hold down both ALT and SHIFT while you rotate an object.

Rotating objects in Publisher is simple and accurate. To quickly rotate an object to any angle from 0 to 360 degrees, perform the steps below:

1 Click the object you want to rotate.

2 Press and hold down the ALT key.

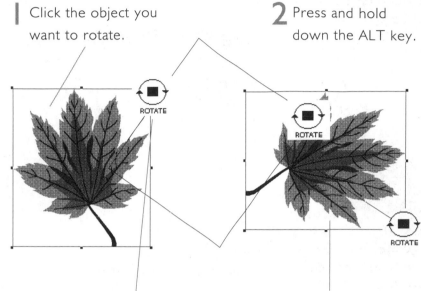

3 Position the mouse pointer on a selection handle. When the mouse pointer symbol changes to the Rotate symbol drag the mouse in the direction you want to rotate.

4 When the object is positioned at the desired angle, release the mouse button and ALT key.

If you want to rotate a group of objects at the same time, make sure all the objects you want to rotate are selected. You can use the multiple object selecting method using the SHIFT key, as described on the previous page.

To unrotate a rotated object

If you want to reverse a rotated object, after selecting the object, open the Arrange menu and choose Rotate or Flip, followed by Custom Rotate. Then click the No Rotation button, followed by the Close button.

Positioning objects precisely

You can position a selected object precisely: first zoom in to the desired object, then hold down ALT while you press the UP, DOWN, LEFT or RIGHT ARROW keys.

You can also display the Custom Rotate dialog box by clicking the Custom Rotate button on the Standard toolbar.

Ruler guides can help you position an object precisely. To drag a ruler guide onto the page, hold down SHIFT while you place the mouse pointer on the horizontal or vertical ruler. When the mouse pointer changes to the 'Adjust' symbol, drag a guide onto the page.

Sometimes, the procedures outlined on the previous page may not provide the precision you need. To rotate an object to a precise angle, select the object, open the Arrange menu and click on Rotate or Flip, then Custom Rotate. Then, in the Custom Rotate dialog box, carry out the following steps:

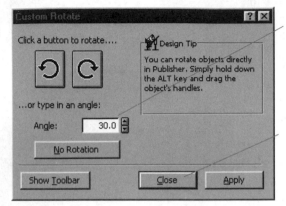

I In the Angle edit box, type in the desired angle.

2 Click the Close button.

Using 'Snap to...'

Publisher uses the term 'snap' to mean 'pull towards something'. The Tools menu contains three commands: Snap to Ruler Marks, Snap to Guides, and Snap to Objects, which can also be used to help align text and graphic objects on the page. When these commands are turned on, Publisher places a tick mark next to the command. To turn the command off, simply click the command on the menu.

- *Snap to Ruler Marks command* – drag the object you want to the desired location as described previously in this chapter, until the edge of the object snaps to the desired ruler mark.

- *Snap to Guides command* – this command works in the same way as Snap to Ruler Marks, except you snap to the desired guide.

- *Snap to Objects command* – drag an object towards the object to which you want to snap. When within snapping range, Publisher snaps the selected object to the destination object.

Centring objects on the page

Publisher provides several options to make the job of centring objects on the page easy. To quickly align objects together, first hold down the SHIFT key while you select all the objects you want to align. Then, choose Align Objects from the Arrange menu. You can then enter your options in the Align Objects dialog box, as shown below:

To draw an object from its centre outwards, press and hold down the CTRL key before you choose the desired drawing tool. Next, draw your shape and then release the mouse button before releasing the CTRL key.

You can also move objects in small steps by using the Nudge command in the Arrange menu. To change the nudge distance, in the Nudge dialog box, click the 'Nudge by' box and enter the desired nudge value into the 'Nudge by' edit box, then click the Close button.

2 Click the 'Align along margins' check box to add a tick mark.

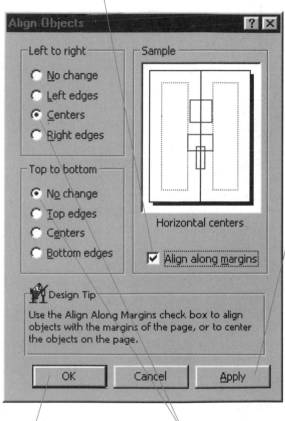

3 (Optional) To see the true effect of your choices before confirming, click the Apply button and drag the dialog box away from the page centre.

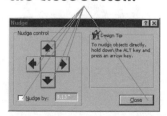

4 Click OK.

1 Click on the desired options in the Left to Right category and the Top to Bottom category.

Creating a mirror image of an object

Publisher provides a wide range of tools to help you create attractive and interesting publications. For example, sometimes you may want to create an eye-catching effect by including two objects which display as mirror images of each other. You can easily create a mirror image of any shape or line created in Publisher with the drawing tools.

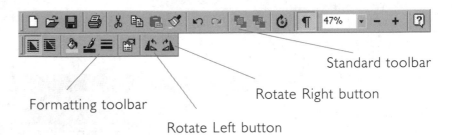

Standard toolbar

Rotate Right button

Formatting toolbar

Rotate Left button

You can mirror an object horizontally or vertically. Carry out the following steps to mirror or 'flip' a desired object or multiple selected objects:

1 Make a copy of the object you want to mirror.

2 Click the object you want to mirror with the Pointer tool to select it.

3 Directly below the Standard toolbar, on the Formatting toolbar, click the Rotate Left button or the Rotate Right button (shown above).

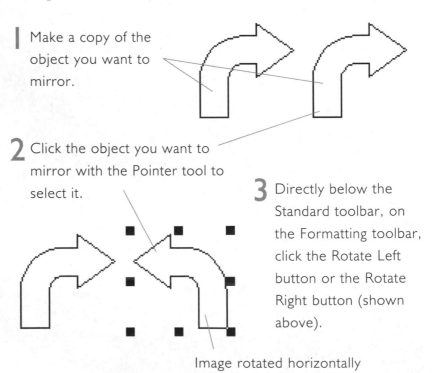

Image rotated horizontally

Grouping and ungrouping objects

 Another way to select objects you want to group is to press and hold down the SHIFT key while you click on them individually.

Sometimes, you may want to work with several objects at the same time, without disturbing the position or spacing of the individual objects in relation to each other. Wouldn't it be great if these objects could be treated as a single item while you move, resize or rotate the group in a single action? You can do this in Publisher using a procedure known as grouping.

To group and ungroup several objects, perform the following steps:

1 Hold down the left mouse button and drag a selection box around the objects you want to group.

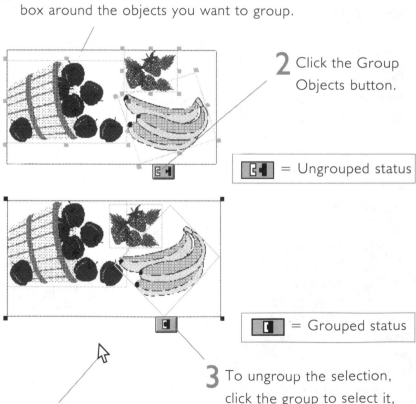

 Even though objects may be grouped, you can still change the border, shading or text of any individual object. First, click the object you want to affect. Then choose the desired command.

2 Click the Group Objects button.

= Ungrouped status

= Grouped status

 To identify at a glance if an object is grouped, look at the selection handles. Grouped objects have one set of selection handles around the group.

3 To ungroup the selection, click the group to select it, then click the Group Objects button again.

4 Click anywhere outside of the selection to clear the boundary box.

Layering objects

You can also change the layering of more than one object at a time, by first selecting all the objects you want to change. (To do this, hold down the SHIFT key while you click each object you want.)

To create the illusion of depth, you can place several overlapping objects on a page. The last object placed appears to be closest to us, while the first object placed seems furthest away, and so on. Publisher refers to this condition as layering, and we refer to the layered objects collectively as the 'stack'.

Top of the stack   Middle of the stack   Bottom of the stack

To ensure text or pictures appear behind all objects on every page in your publication, place the objects you want on the background (see page 30).

You can change the order of layered objects by following the steps below:

1 Click the object you want to change.

To overlay text onto another object, drag out a text frame, type and format your text, then place it in front of the object. Arrange the order of layering. To see the object through the text frame, select the text frame and click CTRL+T

2 Open the Arrange menu and choose one of the following commands, depending on what you want to do:

- Bring to Front
- Bring Forward
- Send Backward
- Send to Back

Applying and changing borders

To delete a border entirely, first click the object whose border you want to delete. Next, click the Line/Border Style button on the Formatting toolbar. Finally, click the None command on the floating menu.

Borders are great for making a picture stand out, or teasing the eye towards an object, or even as design elements in their own right. You can easily add, modify or delete a border around a text or graphic object. Furthermore, with rectangular borders, you can change the colour and thickness of the individual sides. Therefore, to add a border around an object, first click the object to select it. Then carry out the steps below:

Publisher applies a border inside a frame. Therefore, avoid making the thickness of a border too wide. If a border is too wide, graphic objects may become compressed or some text in a text frame may become hidden.

1 On the Formatting toolbar, click the Line/ Border Style button.

2 You can quickly apply a border simply by clicking the desired line on the floating menu.

3 Alternatively, you can see more borders by clicking the More Styles command, to display the Border Style dialog box.

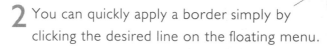

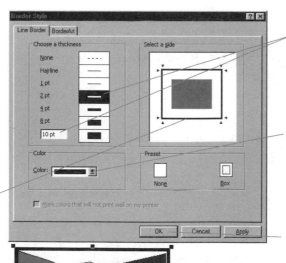

4 Click the desired line thickness, or type a value in the edit box.

To change an individual side of a border, after step 3, click the side you want here. Then optionally perform steps 4 and 5. Finally, click the OK button.

5 (Optional) Click another colour from the drop-down list.

6 Click OK.

The object at the top of this page with the new border applied

Making an object transparent

Another way in which you can add interest, contrast and sparkle to a document is to change the default fill of objects. In Publisher, all objects you create – including frames – have a default fill status. Usually this is set to 'transparent'. You can build up a design that is perhaps made up of several individually drawn elements containing various fill colours, tints and pattern styles. Sometimes, you can further enhance a design by selectively making objects transparent, as shown below:

 If the apply transparent /opaque operation does not appear to work, you may be trying to work on an image imported from another application. The action works only with objects which originate in Publisher.

If your document may be used as part of a Web site, think carefully about applying a pattern or gradient fill to a text frame. When you publish to the Web, Publisher converts this type of text frame to a graphic, and so will take longer for users to download.

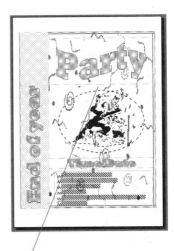

1 Select the object you want to make transparent.

2 Press CTRL+T, to switch the state. Each time you press CTRL+T, the state toggles.

If you apply CTRL+T to a piece of selected clip art, only the clip art background transparent/opaque status is changed, not the clip art itself. Some attractive designs can be created using this technique.

Several objects can be affected at once by holding down SHIFT while you click each object you want to make transparent. Alternatively, draw a selection box around all the objects you want to change to select the entire group, then apply the steps above.

Making an object opaque

Making an object opaque is of course simply the reverse of making an object transparent, except that you have a choice of which style of opaqueness – or fill – to apply. You can change not only the colour of the fill but also the pattern.

To make an object opaque and apply a fill, carry out the following steps:

 If you click the Apply button in the Colors and Fill Effects dialog boxes, you can see the effects of your choices before actually making them. Note, the dialog box may be blocking your view, so you may need to drag the Title bar to move it away.

 To quickly make a transparent selected object opaque, and apply the default fill, simply press CTRL+T.

Select the transparent object you want to make opaque.

2 Click the Fill Color button near the Formatting toolbar.

3 On the Colors Palette, click on the colour you want to apply.

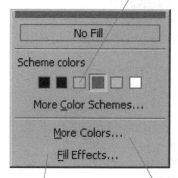

4 To see more colour choices, click the More Colors button, then click your desired colour followed by the OK button.

5 To apply a shade, tint, pattern or gradient, click the Fill Effects button, then click the desired options followed by the OK button.

Applying a shadow

Shadows in Publisher enhance the illusion of depth and can transform a plain shape into something more striking. You can apply a shadow to any shape created with the drawing tools or around frames. To add further specialist shadowed effects to text, you can use the WordArt program that comes with Publisher. To apply a simple shadow to an object, perform the following steps:

To quickly add a shadow to a selected shape (or remove a shadow), press CTRL+D.

The boundaries and guides included in your publication never appear in print. To view your publication without the boundaries and guides shown, simply click 'Hide Boundaries and Guides' in the View menu.

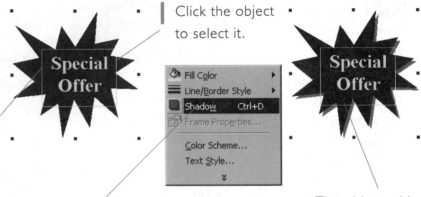

1 Click the object to select it.

2 On the Format menu, click the Shadow command.

The object with shadow applied

When creating a custom shape, if you can't see the top shape, you may have formatted it as transparent. Press CTRL+T to quickly change it to opaque.

Removing an applied shadow

You can remove a shadow by applying the steps above to an object that already has a shadow. Alternatively, use the Undo Shadow command in the Edit menu if it is available.

Creating a custom shadow

Sometimes, Publisher may not produce the exact shadow shape you want. By default, Publisher always creates a grey-coloured shadow of a set depth. To create a unique shadow, first create the shape to which you want to apply a shadow. Using the Copy and Paste commands in the Edit menu, make a copy of the selected shape and paste it on the page. Apply the desired fill to the first shape and then to the shadow shape. Finally, place the first shape in front of the shadow shape and adjust to create the desired shadow effect. Remember, you can use the Send... and Bring... commands in the Arrange menu.

Using Object Linking & Embedding

 Not all programs are OLE-compatible. To view a list of all the programs on your system that are OLE-compatible, click Object in the Insert menu, and use the scroll bar to view the contents of the Object Type box.

 Embed an object when you're the only person working on the publication, so that any changes you make to the contents of an embedded object affect only that publication.

 Link an object if you're sharing it with other people or other documents. Then, any changes made to the content of the object can be reflected wherever that object exists.

Objects can be created in other programs and included in a Publisher document. For example, you might want to use a chart created in Microsoft Excel. Furthermore, a linked object maintains a link to its original source program. Often, the information used to form these objects may change, and so you need a method to make sure these objects can be updated easily, even if already placed in a Publisher document. The answer is provided by an enhancement called Object Linking and Embedding (OLE), which may be included in the software.

OLE ensures that if any such objects are placed within a Publisher document, you can start up the source program from within Publisher to edit the object using the tools from the source program – without leaving Publisher. For this to work, however, you must first link or embed the desired object in a Publisher document, and also, the source program must be OLE-compatible.

Linking or embedding an object

To link or embed an object, first make sure no other object is selected in Publisher. Then carry out the steps below:

1 Open the Insert menu and click the Object command.

2 Click Create from File.

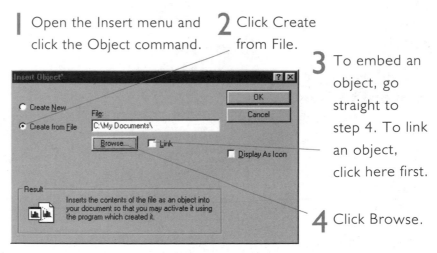

3 To embed an object, go straight to step 4. To link an object, click here first.

4 Click Browse.

5 In the Browse dialog box, navigate through the folders to find the file you want to link/embed, and click that file to select it. Click the Insert button.

6 Click OK.

After Publisher has created the new linked or embedded object, you can move and resize the object as described earlier in this chapter.

Updating a linked object

To update the link to an object in your publication, first open the Edit menu and click Links. Then carry out the steps below:

To change a link, first open the Edit menu and click Links. Next, in the list of linked objects, click the object whose link you want to change. Click the Change Source button, followed by the file to which you want to link. Finally, click OK, followed by Close.

1 In the list of linked objects, click the object you want to update.

4 Click Cancel.

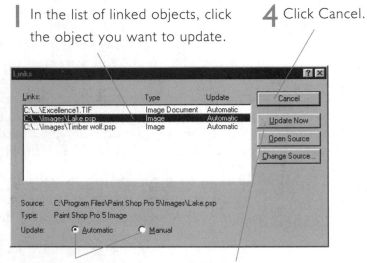

2 Click either Automatic or Manual for the method of update.

3 Click Update Now. If the object is already up-to-date, this button may be shown greyed-out (unavailable).

Editing a linked or embedded object

To edit a linked or embedded object, first double-click the desired object. Next, make your changes using the source program's tools. To return to Publisher, click the Exit or Exit and Return command in the source program's File menu, followed by clicking Yes if prompted to save. However, if you can only see the Publisher Title bar, simply click outside the object workspace to return to Publisher proper.

Drawing simple shapes

This chapter explores how you can create and modify lines, rectangles, circles and other simple geometrical shapes using the drawing tools in the Objects toolbar. You can also discover how to create more complex shapes using Microsoft Draw.

Covers

Chapter Four

Working with lines and arrows

 To give 'depth' to a line, first click on it with the right mouse button. Then choose the Change Line command followed by the Shadow command.

 To create a fancy line, first draw a narrow box with the Box tool. Then click the Line/Border Style button on the Formatting toolbar, followed by the More Styles command. Click the BorderArt tab and choose your border. Click OK to finish.

 To draw a straight line precisely, hold down the SHIFT key while you draw the line. Or press the CTRL key to draw a straight line precisely from the centre outwards.

Lines can help give emphasis to, and separate, information within a document. In Publisher you can choose from a range of line styles and types, from plain lines and arrowhead lines to Fancy lines – which are lines made up of individual elements using the BorderStyle dialog box. To draw a simple line, perform the steps below:

1 Click the Line tool [ ] on the Objects toolbar.

2 Place the mouse pointer where you want the line to begin and drag the mouse to create the desired line length.

3 (Optional) If you want to convert the line to an arrow, click the desired Arrow button on the Formatting toolbar.

Add/Remove...
...Left Arrow   ...Right Arrow
...Both Arrows

4 (Optional) If you want to choose a different line style or see further arrow options, click the right mouse button over the selected line, then choose Change Line, followed by Line/ Border Style then More Styles. Choose your desired options and click OK.

Note: you can delete a selected line simply by pressing the DELETE key.

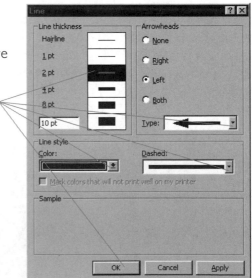

Drawing a rectangle

The box or rectangle shape is one of the most common components used in page design. You can draw rectangles easily using the Rectangle tool on the Objects toolbar. To create depth and added impact, you could simply add another box in the form of a shadow box. To draw a simple rectangle, carry out the following steps:

 To draw a precise square, hold down the SHIFT key as you drag the mouse diagonally.

1 Click the Rectangle tool 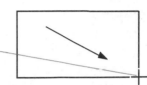 on the Objects toolbar.

2 Place the mouse pointer where you want the uppermost left corner to start, then drag down diagonally towards the right.

3 When you see the desired box shape, release the mouse button.

 To draw a rectangle from the centre outwards, hold down the CTRL key as you drag the mouse diagonally.

Drawing a fancy rectangle

To create a more striking box with a fancy border, first click inside the existing box with the right mouse button. Then perform the following steps on the selected box:

1 Click Change Rectangle, followed by Line/Border Style, followed by More Styles.

 To draw a precise square from the centre outwards, hold down both the SHIFT and CTRL keys as you drag the mouse diagonally.

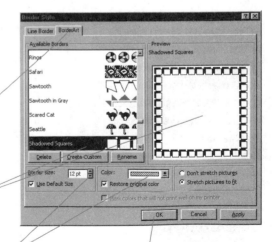

2 Click the BorderArt tab.

3 Click a new border style.

4 (Optional) Type in a new border thickness and colour.

5 Click the OK button to make your changes.

Drawing an oval/circle

You can draw any variety of oval shape or a precise circle using the Oval tool on the Objects toolbar. Carry out the following steps to draw an oval or circle:

 Any shape you create with the drawing tools is an object. Therefore, you can change the size and proportion of any drawn shape by dragging the selection handles, as described in Chapter 3.

 The Measurements toolbar can help you create and position objects precisely. To display the Measurements toolbar, with the right mouse button, click on any empty space on the Desktop and choose the Toolbars command, followed by the Measurements command.

1 Click the Oval tool on the Objects toolbar:

2 Place the mouse pointer at the location where you want the upper-left of the oval or circle to be, then drag down diagonally. To draw a perfect circle, hold down the SHIFT key as you drag the mouse.

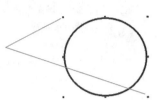

3 When you see the desired shape, release the mouse button.

As with any shape you create with the drawing tools, you can change the outline colour, type and size, in addition to changing the object fill. These aspects are examined later in this chapter. But for now, let's take a quick look at how you can hide part of a drawn oval (or any other object).

Hiding part of an oval (or any other object)

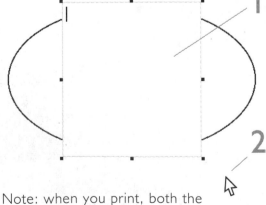

1 With the Text tool, draw a shape directly on top of the oval, so that it covers the part you want hidden.

2 Click outside of the selection to hide the selection handles.

Note: when you print, both the text frame and the hidden part of the object will not be seen

Drawing a custom shape

Included as part of the drawing tools are 36 predesigned common shapes. You can see all of these shapes when you click the Custom Shapes tool on the Objects toolbar. To apply a custom shape, follow the procedure outlined below:

1 On the Objects toolbar, click the Custom Shapes tool to display the fly-out custom shapes menu.

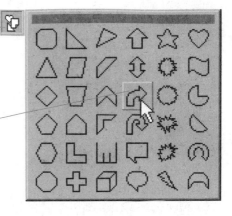

2 Click the desired shape.

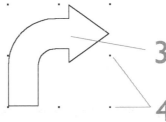

3 Click where you want the shape to appear.

4 Adjust the size, position and proportions of the shape as desired.

Modifying the shape of a custom shape

Some custom shapes contain Adjust handles when placed. You can modify the shape as shown below:

 Some custom shapes don't have Adjust handles. Therefore, these shapes can only be resized by dragging a selection handle.

1 Click the desired custom shape.

2 Place the mouse pointer on an Adjust handle (a grey diamond within the perimeter of the shape's selection handles).

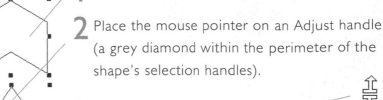

3 When the mouse pointer symbol changes to the Adjust symbol, drag the mouse to modify the shape as desired.

Changing the border

When you first draw a shape, Publisher applies a default border of a 1-point-thick plain black line. However, you can change the border style, thickness and colour, or even remove the border entirely. If you've drawn a box, you can even apply a fancy border using the Line/Border Style button on the Formatting toolbar. Follow the steps below to change the border of a shape:

To remove a border entirely from a shape or an object, first click the shape to select it. Then click the Line/Border Style button on the Formatting toolbar, followed by the None command.

1 After clicking the shape to select it, click the Line/Border Style button on the Formatting toolbar: ≡

2 On the floating menu, click More Styles.

3 In the Border dialog box, click a new preset thickness or type another value in the Edit box. For box shapes, you can change each side individually.

If your shape is a rectangle or box, you can replace a plain border with a fancy border. First click the shape to select it. Next, click the Line/Border Style button, followed by the More Styles command. Click the BorderArt tab, then choose your desired border settings and click the OK button.

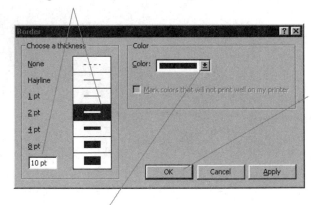

5 Click OK to confirm your changes.

4 (Optional) Click another colour from the drop-down list. For box shapes, you can click each side to change its colour.

The above shape with a new border size and colour applied

Changing the fill colour

Publisher is rich in options which enable you to apply a different fill to a shape. Publisher gives every shape you draw a default fill colour and pattern. You can change colours, choose from a variety of patterns, or change both the colour and the pattern. To change the fill colour, perform the following steps:

1 Click the shape whose colour you want to change to select it.

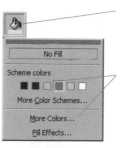

2 Click the Fill Color button on the Formatting toolbar.

3 On the Colors Palette, click on the colour you want. But if you can't see the desired colour, click the More Colors button.

4 Click your desired colour, then OK. If you can't see the colour you want, go to step 5.

6 Click an area of the colour chart or enter values in the edit boxes.

5 Define your own custom colour: click All colors.

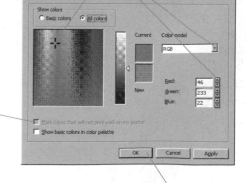

7 (Optional) Click here to let Publisher show you which colour combinations may not print well on your printer (see DON'T FORGET icon in the margin).

8 Click OK.

Changing the fill pattern

Fill patterns in Publisher can provide a stunning and powerful focus to an object. You can apply tints/shades, patterns and graduated fills – or gradients, as they are referred to in Publisher. To change the fill pattern of a shape, first click the shape you want to change to select it. Then perform the following steps:

 If you plan to use graduated fills in your publication, it's a good idea to make some test prints as soon as possible. Some printers can't handle some graduated fills and patterns easily, and therefore may substitute a chosen colour with a solid colour, or even black.

1 On the Formatting toolbar, click the Fill Color button.

2 On the Colors Palette, click the Fill Effects button.

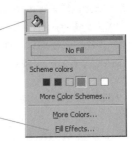

3 Choose the options you want to apply. Use the scroll bar to see more.

4 (Optional) Click a base colour and a second colour.

Note: Publisher provides a sample of your choice here. Click the Apply button to see the effect on your page.

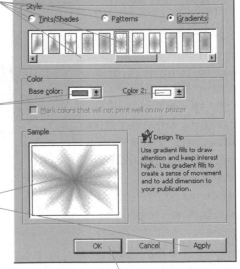

5 Click OK to apply your new patterns and shading options.

The object above with the new shading applied

Using Microsoft Draw

To quickly learn how to use Microsoft Draw, immediately after starting Draw, press the F1 key to bring up an excellent range of Help topics.

Microsoft Draw is a Windows-based drawing program that now comes bundled with Publisher. So any time you want to create a picture that calls for more complex input than is available in Publisher, you can simply open the Insert menu and choose the Picture command followed by New Drawing to start Microsoft Draw.

By default, the Drawing and AutoShapes toolbars then appear and the commands available in the Standard and Formatting toolbars change to include the new necessary functions, as shown in the Microsoft Draw window below.

You can also start Microsoft Draw by opening the Insert menu and choosing the Object command. Then in the dialog box that follows, choose Create New followed by Microsoft Draw Drawing and click OK.

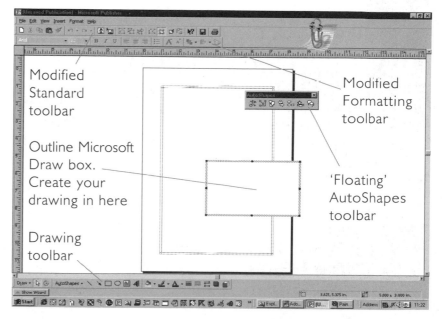

Modified Standard toolbar

Outline Microsoft Draw box. Create your drawing in here

Drawing toolbar

Modified Formatting toolbar

'Floating' AutoShapes toolbar

You can add text to any AutoShape and change the formatting of the text.

The nice thing about Microsoft Draw now is that you don't need to exit Publisher to use the program – it opens in the current Publisher window.

AutoShapes

Microsoft Draw comes with its own range of pre-drawn shapes. You can modify and manipulate these AutoShapes in a range of ways – eg, resize, rotate, re-texture, combine with other shapes and even fill with pictures, and so on.

To draw a symmetrical Microsoft Draw-related shape, press and hold down the SHIFT key before dragging on a corner selection handle to display the desired size.

 If you make changes to a drawing, but then decide you don't want to keep those changes, immediately click the Undo command on the Edit menu.

 Once you've created a drawing in Microsoft Draw, when you move back into the Publisher window, you can position and manipulate the Microsoft Draw object like any other object (see Chapter 3 for more information).

Creating an object in Microsoft Draw

Carry out the following steps to create an object in Microsoft Draw:

1 Open the Insert menu and choose the Picture command followed by New Drawing.

2 The Microsoft Draw-related toolbars appear in the Publisher window. Start creating your drawing inside the highlighted box.

3 When finished, click outside of the highlighted box and anywhere in the Publisher window to close Microsoft Draw and view your drawing on the page.

Editing an object created in Microsoft Draw

Carry out the following steps to make changes to, or update, an object created in Microsoft Draw:

1 If the drawing you want to edit is already displayed on the Publisher page, double-click the drawing to open the Microsoft Draw window. A highlighted box appears around the object.

2 If the drawing you want to edit is displayed in the Microsoft Draw window, simply select the object or double-click on the object frame (depending on what you want to do) and then edit as desired.

3 When you have finished editing the object, click anywhere outside of the highlighted box in the Publisher window to close Microsoft Draw and view your finished object.

You can create some stunning effects by applying the 3D and Shadow buttons on the Drawing toolbar to a selected Microsoft Draw object.

Working with words

Your choice and use of words can shape the mood and tone of a publication, can persuade and entertain, and can utimately hold or lose your readers' attention. In this chapter, we explore how to insert and manipulate text in a publication and how to change the look of text to create the finish you want.

Chapter Five

Covers

Importing text files

If you're working with multi-page documents containing mostly text, you may decide the job of preparing text for use in Publisher is easier if most of the typing is completed in your favourite word-processor. Publisher can accept text saved in a variety of common word-processor formats, including Microsoft Word, WordPerfect and Rich Text Format (RTF).

If you import or type more text than the target text frame can hold, Publisher stores the excess text in an invisible holding area. To ensure all text is made visible, first click the text frame to select it. Next, open the Format menu and choose AutoFit Text. Finally, from the fly-out menu choose either ẞest Fit or Shrink Text On Overflow.

When you're compiling text from various sources, you may be dealing with text from several different formats. If your contributors cannot save their text files in a Publisher-compatible format, the safest option is to ask them to save in RTF format, which will keep most of the original formatting information. To import a text file into Publisher, carry out the steps below:

1 If you're inserting text into a new location, draw a text frame with the Text Frame tool. If you're inserting text into an existing frame, click where you want the new text to start.

2 Open the Insert menu and click Text File.

3 (Optional) If you can't see the text file you want, click an option to help locate it.

7 If the text won't fit, click Yes to tell Publisher to automatically reflow excess text into new frames.

To turn off automatic copyfitting, follow the same procedure as above, except choose the None command from the fly-out menu.

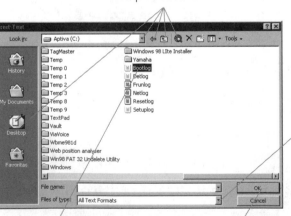

4 (Optional) Click here to see the range of compatible file formats.

5 Click the desired text file.

6 Click OK.

Entering text at the keyboard

If the amount of text is too large to fit in a text frame, you can apply three common solutions: (1) reflow the text to another frame; (2) enlarge an existing text frame; or (3) reduce the text size (see the HOT TIP on the facing page).

The easiest way to create text in your documents is to draw a text frame and simply begin typing. Also, you can easily mix imported text with text you type; simply click where you want to start typing and begin. If the text appears too small because you're seeing your publication in full page view, with the text cursor flashing, press F9 to zoom in to actual size.

When you start typing, Publisher applies a default text size and formatting characteristics. You can change the text size, font, style and alignment later if you wish. Alternatively, you can apply these changes as soon as possible to get a better idea of how much space you'll need. Changing text formatting is examined later in this chapter.

If you're new to keyboard typing

When you begin typing, you don't need to press the ENTER key at the end of every line: Publisher automatically wraps the text to the following line. When you want to start a new line or paragraph, simply press the ENTER key. To indent a line, press the TAB key at the start of a new line. If you make a typing mistake, simply press the BACKSPACE key to erase the last character typed.

Editing in Microsoft Word

Different fonts of the same point size can take up varying amounts of space.

If you have Microsoft Word version 6.0 or later installed on you PC or network, you can use Word to make your editing changes while working in your text frame in Publisher, and then return to your document to bring in the latest changes and updates, as follows:

1 With the right mouse button, click inside a text frame.

2 In the floating menu, click Change Text, followed by Edit Story in Microsoft Word.

3 Edit your text in Word, then click Close and Return in Microsoft Word's File menu to return to your text frame.

Changing a font

Publisher comes with a wide range of different fonts and font styles. To recap, a font is a set of specific characters in a single typeface containing upper and lower case characters, punctuation marks and digits. To change the current font, perform the following steps:

Select the text you want to change by highlighting it. One way to do this is to click the mouse pointer to the left of the first character in the text you want. Then drag across all the text you want to select, and release the mouse button.

 If the fonts in the Font box don't include what you want, you can install other fonts. See your Windows documentation for further information.

 To quickly highlight all text in a text frame, click inside the desired text frame and press CTRL+A. This is the keyboard shortcut for the Highlight Entire Story command in the Edit menu.

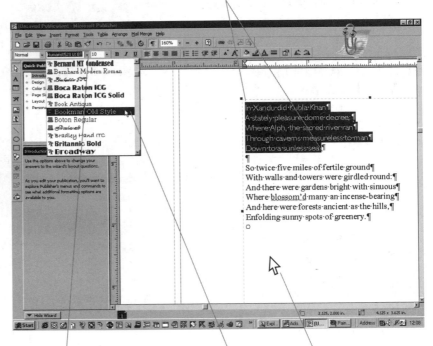

2 In the Font box on the Formatting toolbar, click the drop-down list box arrow to open the font list.

3 Click the desired font in the font list.

4 Click anywhere in the text frame to clear the highlight.

Changing text alignment

 Justified text alignment applied to short text lines or lines containing large fonts can cause gap patterns or "rivers" of unsightly white space running down the page. To avoid this, use smaller font sizes and longer lines of text.

 To change the alignment of an entire block of text, select the entire block before choosing a text alignment button.

 To align text vertically in its frame, first click the desired text frame. Then open the Format menu and choose Align Text Vertically. Finally click Top, Center, or Bottom.

The way in which text is aligned within margins affects readability, and the impact that it makes. Publisher provides four ways to align text: flush left, flush right, centre and justified. By default, when you first create a text frame and begin typing, flush left alignment applies.

Considering text alignment options

Flush left alignment ensures that all lines in a text block align at the left margin, while flush right does the same at the right margin. Centred alignment centres each text line equally between the margins. Justified alignment spaces each text line equally between the margins.

Many people agree that text is easiest to read when aligned flush left (like this book). Flush right aligned text has a ragged left edge and consequently affects readability considerably. Not surprisingly, this is used sparingly.

However, flush right alignment can provide a refreshing alternative when used with consideration. For example, letterheads containing names and addresses, company logos, pull quotes, and so on, can look distinctive and stylish when aligned at the right edge.

Centred alignment is ideal for headings, invitations and announcements; whereas justified alignment can provide a noticeable element of neatness, if the line width is wide and the font size reasonably small. To change text alignment, perform the following steps:

1 Click in the text frame containing the text you want to change (also see the HOT TIP in the margin).

2 Click one of the buttons on the Formatting toolbar shown below.

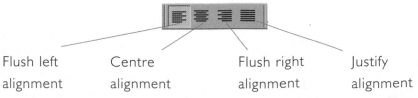

Flush left alignment   Centre alignment   Flush right alignment   Justify alignment

Changing the look of text

You can draw subtle or blatant attention to words or phrases by making the desired text **bold**, *italic*, or ***both***. However, too much of either and the attention-gathering device ceases to work. Choose italics when you want to provide 'medium' emphasis, rather than underlining, to prevent the descenders of letters being 'cut off'.

To quickly remove bold or italic formatting, highlight the desired text and click the appropriate button on the Formatting toolbar.

You can also change emphasis by changing text colour; using more surrounding white space; or by applying considered use of small capitals. To directly change the look of text, perform the steps below:

1 Highlight the text you want to change.

2 To make text bold, click the Bold button.

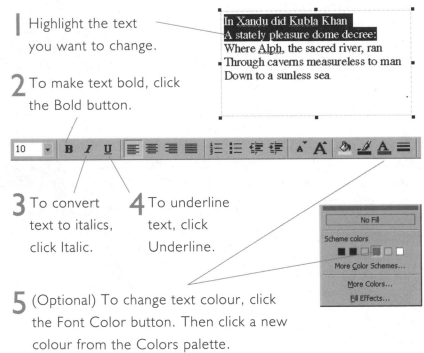

To change text to small capitals LIKE THIS, first select the text you want to change. Next, open the Format menu and click the Font command. In the dialog box, under the Effects category, click Small Caps to add a tick mark. Finish by clicking the OK button.

3 To convert text to italics, click Italic.

4 To underline text, click Underline.

5 (Optional) To change text colour, click the Font Color button. Then click a new colour from the Colors palette.

Changing multiple text properties quickly

If you want to change several text format properties at the same time, first highlight the desired text. Then click the right mouse button over the highlighted text and choose the Change Text followed by the Font command from the floating menu. You can then choose the desired options as described on the following page.

| Click here if you want to choose another font.

4 Click here to underline text.

3 Click here if you want to change the text style: Regular, Italic, Bold, or Bold Italic.

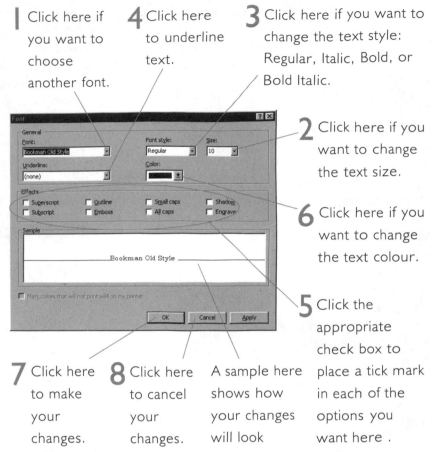

2 Click here if you want to change the text size.

6 Click here if you want to change the text colour.

To quickly remove all the formatting changes made to highlighted text, press CTRL+SPACEBAR.

You can apply more specialised effects to text, using the WordArt program that comes with Publisher. See page 88 for more information.

7 Click here to make your changes.

8 Click here to cancel your changes.

A sample here shows how your changes will look

5 Click the appropriate check box to place a tick mark in each of the options you want here .

Making light text on a dark background

If you want to contrast light text on a dark background, first click in the desired text frame and press CTRL+A.

On the Formatting toolbar, click the Font Color button, then click white from the Colors palette.

Next, also on the Formatting toolbar, click the Fill Color button and choose black from the palette. Lastly, click outside of the selection.

Changing line spacing

Although Publisher automatically applies a default space between adjacent lines of text in each paragraph, you can easily change this value if you wish. However, if the adjustment is too much or too little for the font you're using, readability can become affected. To change line spacing, first click in the paragraph you want to change, or select all the text you want to affect. Then perform the steps below:

Publisher measures line spacing in inches, centimetres, points or picas. However, until you type in a different unit, Publisher uses 'sp' (current line space) units for values up to 4. If you type in a value higher than 4, Publisher, by default, uses points as the line spacing units.

1 With the right mouse button, click the selected text, then choose Change Text, followed by Line Spacing from the floating menus.

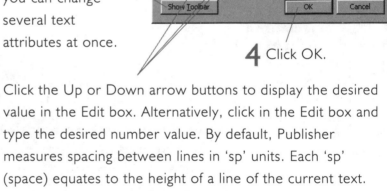

3 (Optional) Click here to display the measurements toolbar in which you can change several text attributes at once.

4 Click OK.

If you want to change the line spacing units, type the appropriate abbreviation for the units you want to use, after entering the desired value in the Edit box: 'in' for inches; 'cm' for centimetres; 'pt' for points; or 'pi' for picas.

2 Click the Up or Down arrow buttons to display the desired value in the Edit box. Alternatively, click in the Edit box and type the desired number value. By default, Publisher measures spacing between lines in 'sp' units. Each 'sp' (space) equates to the height of a line of the current text. Therefore, if you want to apply two line spaces between each line of text, enter 2 here, then press TAB.

Affecting a single line only

If you want the line spacing change to affect a single line only, press ENTER before and after the desired line, to turn the line into a separate paragraph. Then apply the procedure described above.

Changing paragraph spacing

On the previous page, we examined how you can change the line-to-line spacing in a paragraph. In this section, we explore how you can change the amount of space between paragraphs.

You can increase or decrease the amount of space before and after a paragraph. To change the default paragraph-to-paragraph spacing, first click in the paragraph you want to affect, or select all the paragraphs you want to affect. Then perform the steps below:

Publisher measures paragraph spacing in inches, centimetres, points or picas.

If you want to change the paragraph spacing units, type the appropriate abbreviation for the units you want to use, after entering the desired value in the Edit box: 'in' for inches; 'cm' for centimetres; 'pt' for points; or 'pi' for picas.

1 Click the selected text with the right mouse button then choose Change Text, followed by Line Spacing from the floating menus.

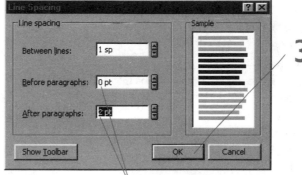

3 Click OK to apply your changes.

2 In the Before Paragraphs box or the After Paragraphs box, click the Up or Down arrow buttons to display the desired value in the Edit box. Alternatively, click in the Edit box and type the desired number value. By default, Publisher measures spacing between paragraphs in 'pt' (point) units. To get an idea of size, there are 72 points to an inch (inches rather than centimetres are used here as points and picas are related to measurement in inches). Picas are also sometimes used and a pica is made up of 12 points. Therefore, if you want to apply 8 points after each paragraph, you would enter 8 in the After Paragraphs edit box. Then press TAB.

Copying text

You can copy individual characters, words, sentences, paragraphs, entire text frames including text, and entire pages if desired. Also, if you have another Windows-based application open when Publisher is started, you may be able to copy text from that application to a document in Publisher.

Copying entire text frames

To copy an entire text frame, including its contents, to another location in the current Publisher document, perform the following steps:

Here's another way to quickly copy a text frame and its contents (or any other object). First, click inside the text frame to select it. Then, place the mouse pointer on the edge of the frame until you see the Move symbol. Hold down CTRL then drag the text frame. When you release the mouse button, Publisher then creates an identical copy.

1 With the right mouse button, click in the text frame you want to copy.

2 From the floating menu, click Copy.

'Please·sir,·I·want·some·more.'¶
The·master·was·a·fat,·healthy·man,·but·
he·turned·very·pale.·He·gazed·in·stupe-
fied·astonishment·on·the·small·rebel·for·
some·seconds,·and·then·clung·for·sup-
port·to·the·copper.·The·assistants·were·
paralysed·with·wonder,·the·boys·with·
fear.¶
'What!'·said·the·master·at·length,·in·a·
faint·voice.¶
'Please·sir'·replied·Oliver,·'I·want·some·
more.'¶
The·master·aimed·a·blow·at·Oliver's·
head·with·a·ladle,·pinioned·him·in·his·
arms,·and·shrieked·aloud·for·the·beadle

Cut
Copy
Paste
Delete Text
Delete Object
Change Text
Change Frame
Proofing Tools
Whole Page
Page Width
Actual Size
Selected Objects
Help on This Text Frame

3 Move to where you want to place your copy. If you're copying to another page, move to the desired page.

5 From the floating menu, click the Paste command.

4 With the right mouse button, click anywhere on free space in the Workspace area.

6 Drag the object to your desired location on the page.

You can then finely adjust the placing of the copied text frame. Also, if you immediately click the Paste command again, you can paste further, multiple copies.

...cont'd

The Copy and Paste commands are also available in the Edit menu. Also, other Windows applications may have Copy and Paste commands in their Edit menus, so you may be able to copy and paste information between Publisher and other applications.

You can copy and paste information between two Publisher documents. In the active document, copy the information you want. Then, open the destination document and paste the copied information where you want it.

Copying partial text

Sometimes, you may want to copy only part of the text in a frame. To do this, first highlight the text you want to copy: one way of doing this is described in step 1 of the procedure on page 62. Then perform the following steps:

1 With the right mouse button, click over the highlighted text.

2 From the floating menu, click Copy.

port·to·the·copper.·The·assistants·were· paralysed·with·wonder,·the·boys·with· fear.¶
'What!'·said·the·master·at·length,·in·a· faint·voice.¶
'Please·sir'·replied·Oliver,·'I·want·so more.'¶
The·master·aimed·a·blow·at·Oliver's· head·with·a·ladle,·pinioned·him·in·his· arms,·and·shrieked·aloud·for·the·bead

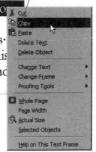

3 Move to where you want to copy your text. If you're copying to another page, move to the desired page.

4 To finish, perform either step 5 or step 6. If you want to insert the copied text into an existing text frame, go to step 5. If you want to insert the copied text into a new text frame, go to step 6.

5 With the left mouse button, click where you want to insert your text. Then, with the right mouse button, click inside the frame. Finally, from the floating menu, click the Paste command.

6 With the right mouse button, click any blank area of the page (containing no objects). Then from the floating menu, click the Paste command.

Moving text

 To move highlighted text or an entire text frame to another document or Windows application, remember you may be able to use the Cut and Paste commands in the Edit menu in both the source and destination applications.

 When you're moving specific highlighted text using the drag-and-drop feature, place the mouse pointer over the highlighted text, but wait until Publisher changes the mouse pointer symbol to the Drag symbol shown below before dragging the highlighted text.

DRAG

Publisher provides several easy ways in which you can move text around a page; from page to page, and between Publisher documents. The method you use depends on several factors, such as whether you're moving an entire text frame or specific highlighted text. Remember also, you may be able to move text to a document in another application, if the destination application is compatible with Publisher.

To move an entire text frame within a document

1 Click inside the text frame you want to move.

2 Place the mouse pointer on the text frame border until the mouse pointer symbol changes to the Move symbol.

3 Hold down the left mouse button and drag the text frame to the desired location. If you want to move to another page, first place the text frame on the non-printing work area. Move to the desired page. Then, click the text frame and drag it onto the desired page in the same manner.

To move specific text on the same page

1 Highlight the text you want to move. When you see the Drag symbol, drag to another location and release the mouse button.

To move specific text within a document

1 Start by highlighting the text you want to move.

2 With the right mouse button, click on top of the highlighted text to display the floating menu and then choose Cut.

3 Move to where you want to place your cut text. If you're placing the text in an existing paragraph, click where you want to place it. To place your text in a new text frame, with the left mouse button click on a page outside of any objects. Next, with the right mouse button, click the page to display the floating menu. Finally, click the Paste command.

Deleting text

You can delete specific text or an entire text frame easily in Publisher. However, sometimes you may want to delete text in frames but keep the frames in place. The following procedures describe your options when deleting text:

To delete a single character at a time, click where you want to delete. Then, each time you want to delete one character to the left of the insertion point, press the BACKSPACE key.

Each time you want to delete one character to the right of the insertion point, press the DELETE key.

If you accidentally delete text you want to keep, before performing any other action, click the Undo button on the Standard toolbar, or choose the Undo command in the Edit menu.

To delete some but not all text in a frame

1 Highlight the text you want to delete.

2 Press the DELETE key.

To delete an entire text frame and the text within (method 1)

1 Click the right mouse button inside the text frame you want to delete.

2 From the floating menu, click the Delete Object command.

To delete all text in a chain of connected text frames without deleting the frames

1 Click inside one of the text frames in the connected sequence.

2 Press CTRL+A (the shortcut to highlight all text in the chain).

3 Press the DELETE key.

To delete an entire text frame and the text within (method 2)

1 Click inside the text frame you want to delete.

2 Press CTRL+SHIFT+X.

Finding specific text

You can use Publisher's Find command to quickly search for text containing specified characters in the selected text frame. If the text frame you're searching in is part of a connected chain, Publisher searches all the frames in the chain.

By default, Publisher flags all text containing the characters you specify. For example, if you enter the characters 'ate', Publisher will flag 'create', 'date' and 'ate' if these words are present in the text. However, you can tell Publisher to find only exact specific text, if you wish, and limit the search criteria by specifying whether to flag only upper-case or lower-case characters. Carry out the steps below to find the desired text:

Before starting a search, make sure that all text has been flowed into text frames. Publisher can only locate fully flowed text. Any text which cannot be seen because it's located in the 'overflow' area, beyond the bottom of a text frame, will not be searched.

You can easily identify if not all text has been flowed. Look at the Connect frame button at the bottom of each text frame: if it has three small boxes on it, there is more text still to flow.

1 Click the text or table frame in which you want to search.

2 Click the Find command in the Edit menu.

5 (Optional) Click here to limit the search to the exact characters in the 'Find what' box.

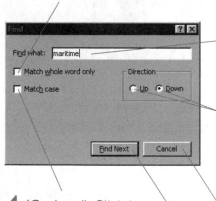

3 Type the characters you want to search for here.

6 (Optional) Click the appropriate option button to search in an upward or downward direction.

4 (Optional) Click here to limit the search to text containing characters in the same case as the text in the 'Find what' box.

8 Click here to end your search.

7 Click here to begin the search.

Replacing text with other text

To delete all instances of the text that you're searching for, simply leave the 'Replace with' edit box blank and click the Replace All button.

If the selected frame is part of a series of connected frames, Publisher will carry out the search and replace sequence in all frames in the chain.

You can tell Publisher to replace all instances of the target text by clicking the Replace All button. However, remember you do lose control of the action, so be sure that this is what you want to do.

In addition to finding text, you can also tell Publisher to replace specific text with other text. If you're not sure of the exact spelling, you can still probably locate the desired text by using the 'wildcard' question mark symbol, as described in the search procedure shown below:

1 Click the frame in which you want to search and replace text.

2 Click Replace in the Edit menu.

3 Type the text you want to find here. Use a question mark for each character you're unsure of.

4 Here, type the text you want to replace the found text with.

5 (Optional) Click here to limit the search to the exact characters in the 'Find what' box.

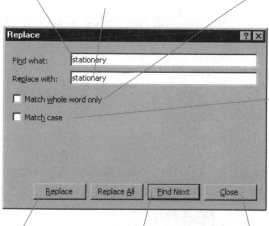

6 (Optional) Click here to limit the search to text containing characters in the same case as the text in the 'Find what' box.

7 Click here to search for the desired text.

8 If Publisher finds the target text, click here to replace it, and go to step 7 again. And so on. Alternatively, click Find Next to ignore the current find and continue the search.

9 Click here to end the search and replace sequence.

Exporting text

When you export text, you're not actually moving a Publisher document, but simply saving a copy in another format.

When you're ready to use the exported text, start up the target application and open the document to where you want to add your exported text. Then use the application's Open, Import, or Insert Text command to place your exported file.

If you want to store your exported publication in another location, use the file buttons to navigate to the desired location before exporting.

There may be occasions when you've created a document in Publisher, but you want to use some or all of the text in another non-Publisher-compatible document.

Publisher can save files in a range of different formats. So, if you're planning to use Publisher text elsewhere, and you know the application in which you expect to continue working on your Publisher-based text, try to save the file in a compatible format if possible.

If you're not sure which application you'll be using, then save the file in RTF format. To export a text file, first make sure that you've saved your file as a Publisher document with the Save As command (see Chapter 2, page 31). Then carry out the steps below:

3 Click here to save and export your document.

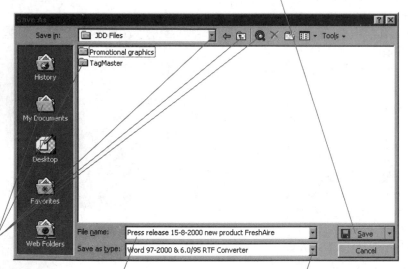

| Type a unique name for the text you're exporting.

2 Click here to view the range of export file formats available and choose one from the list.

Using the advanced text features

Publisher contains some powerful yet easy-to-use text manipulation tools. In this chapter, we examine how to use these tools and how to create some common arrangements like bulleted lists, fancy first letters and indented text blocks.

Chapter Six

Covers

Changing character spacing

To quickly highlight the entire text in a frame, press CTRL+A.

Previously, we've examined how to change the spacing between lines of text and between paragraphs. Publisher also provides commands which enable you to alter the spacing between characters – also known as tracking.

This option can be useful if you want to improve the general look of text or to ensure specific text fits in the available space in a frame. For example, the look of headlines made up of larger font sizes can sometimes be improved by having their character spacing reduced.

When you change character spacing, Publisher makes a 'best guess'. Sometimes, characters may overlap. If this happens, click a looser spacing option in the Character Spacing dialog box.

To change character spacing in a specific paragraph, first highlight the desired paragraph. If you want to affect more than a single paragraph, highlight all the paragraphs you want to change. Then perform the following steps:

1 Open the Format menu and choose the Character Spacing command.

Tight spacing brings letters closer together; loose spacing moves letters further apart.

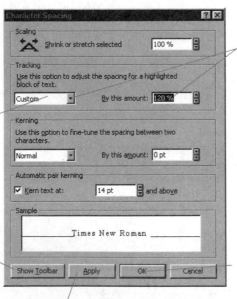

2 Click one of the preset options under the Tracking category (see the DON'T FORGET icon in the margin). Or choose the Custom option here and enter a new value in the By This Amount box (range 0.1% to 600%).

Click here to show the Measurements toolbar, from which you can make multiple text formatting changes.

4 Click OK to make your changes.

3 (Optional) Click here to see (try out) your changes before you make them.

Changing character-pair kerning

To stretch or compress the width of characters, enter a value of between 0.1–600% under the Scaling option in the Character Spacing dialog box.

Kerning is the process of changing the spacing between certain pairs of characters that the human eye would otherwise perceive to be too close together or too far apart. The kerning values used vary from font to font.

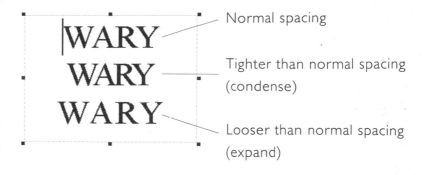

Normal spacing

Tighter than normal spacing (condense)

Looser than normal spacing (expand)

Here's the difference between tracking and kerning. Tracking adjusts the space between characters in a block of text; kerning adjusts the space between certain pairs of characters only.

To change the default kerning settings, first highlight the specific words or letters you want to change. Next, open the Format menu and click the Character Spacing command. Then, in the Character Spacing dialog box, carry out the following steps:

Publisher provides a visual representation of your changes as you make them. Also, you can click the Apply button to test out your proposed changes before confirming with the OK button.

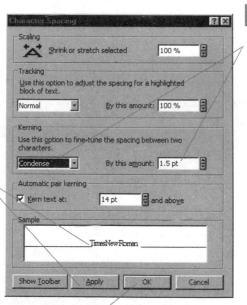

Under the Kerning category, click the option you want here. To increase the amount of space between characters, click Expand. To decrease the amount of space, click Condense. Whichever option you choose, enter a value between 0.1 and 600 in the 'By this amount' box.

2 Click OK to make your changes.

Working with symbols

You can change how a symbol appears by applying normal font formatting to the desired symbol. For example, you can use bold or *italics*.

Often, you may want to include special symbols in your documents, like bullets (•), copyright (©) and trademark (™) (®) symbols, fractions, and so on. Publisher makes the job of including these in your documents easy. To place a symbol into your document, carry out the steps below:

1 In the text/table, click where you want to place the symbol.

2 Open the Insert menu and click the Symbol command.

3 In the Symbol dialog box, click the symbol you want to use.

All symbols available for a specific font are shown in the Symbol dialog box. If the symbol you want is not shown, try choosing another font.

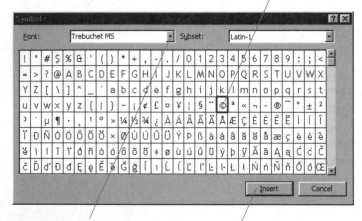

4 (Optional) If the desired symbol is not shown, click here to see other fonts installed on your PC.

5 Click Insert to place the selected symbol on the page or workspace.

Many useful graphic-based symbols are listed under the Wingdings category. You can see these by displaying Wingdings in the Font box in the dialog box.

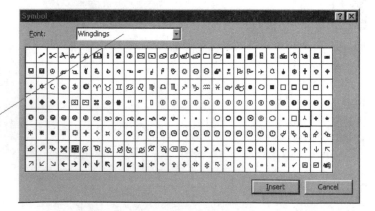

Changing text frame margins

When you draw a text frame, Publisher applies default text margins within the frame. For most purposes, these default settings will probably be adequate. Sometimes however, you may want to change the margins. The following procedure shows you how to alter the size of the text frame margins:

You can enter a margin value for each side individually: Left, Right, Top or Bottom.

If you make the margins too wide, some of your text may seem to disappear. However, the excess text may only have flowed into the hidden overflow area under the text frame. Expand your text frame or create a new text frame and flow the excess text into it.

1 With the right mouse button, click the text frame containing the margins you want to change.

2 On the floating menu, click Change Frame followed by Text Frame Properties.

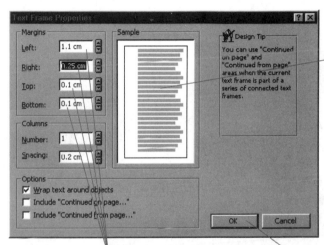

Note: the sample view updates as you enter new values in the Margin boxes

3 In the Text Frame Properties dialog box under the Margins category, enter the desired margin sizes for Left, Right, Top and Bottom margins. You can type in the desired value directly into each box or use the Up/Down buttons to scroll through the preset values. To move to the following field, press TAB.

4 Click OK to make your changes.

Creating a bulleted list

When you want to present information in a clear but loose tabular form, often a bulleted or numbered list is an ideal answer. To create a 'standard' bulleted list, first click where you want to start the list to display the insertion point. If you want to convert existing text to a bulleted list, highlight the text you want to convert first. Then click the Bullets on the Formatting toolbar.

To remove bullets from a list, first highlight the list. Next, click the right mouse button over the highlighted list and choose Change Text followed by Indents and Lists. Under the Indents Settings category, choose Normal, then click OK.

To create a customized bulleted list, after highlighting the text you want as described in the previous paragraph, perform these steps:

1 On the Format menu, choose the Indents and Lists command.

2 Click Bulleted list.

3 Click the bullet type you want.

To quickly create a bulleted list, first type an * (asterisk) followed by a space or tab and then type the text for your first line and press ENTER. You can then continue to type the remaining entries for your list.

4 (Optional) If you can't see the symbol you want, click the New Bullet button and choose another font under the Font category.

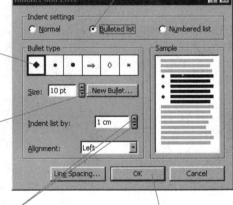

5 (Optional) You can change the indent distance here.

6 Click OK.

7 Type the text for your first line if you've not already done so. Then, each time you want to start a new line with a bullet, press ENTER. To start a new line without inserting a bullet, press SHIFT+ENTER. To end, press ENTER twice.

Creating a numbered list

Numbered lists provide similar benefits to bulleted lists, except that a numbered list implies steps in a procedure or a hierarchy of priorities.

To create a numbered list, first click where you want to start the list to display the insertion point. If you want to convert existing text to a numbered list, highlight the text you want to convert first. Then simply click the Numbering button on the Formatting toolbar.

 To remove numbering from a list, first highlight the list. Next, click the right mouse button over the highlighted list and choose Change Text followed by Indents and Lists. Under the Indents Settings category, choose Normal, then click OK.

To create a customized numbered list, after highlighting the text you want as described in the previous paragraph, then perform these steps:

1 On the Format menu, choose the Indents and Lists command.

2 Click Numbered list.

3 Click the numbering format you want.

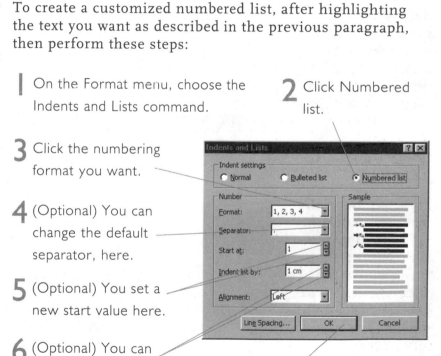

4 (Optional) You can change the default separator, here.

5 (Optional) You set a new start value here.

6 (Optional) You can change the indent distance here.

7 Click OK.

8 Type the text for your first line. Each time you want to start a new line press ENTER. To start a new line without inserting a number, press SHIFT+ENTER. To end, press ENTER twice.

Working with tab stops

Tab stops help you accurately place and align text vertically at specific positions in a text frame, and are particularly useful if you're dealing with tabular information. To indent text precisely and ensure that your printouts are accurate, it's important to use tab stops or indents rather than try to use the SPACEBAR. To set tab stops, first highlight the text you want to set up. Then perform the following steps:

If you prefer, you can insert, edit and delete tabs singly or in multiples, by using the Tabs command in the Format menu to display the Tabs dialog box.

The above example uses the default left tab alignment. This means that Publisher aligns the tabs vertically at the left edge of the words.

Tab Alignment button

On the ruler, click where you want tab stops to appear. Publisher indicates tabs with a marker.

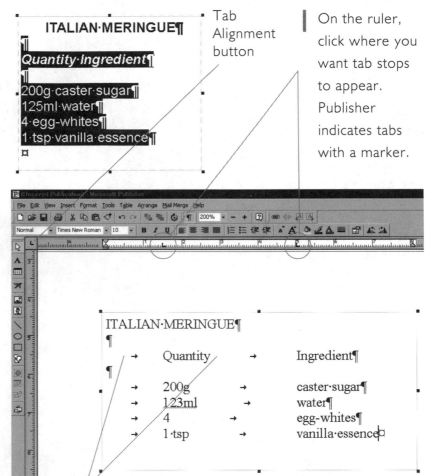

2 On the first text line, click in the text where you want to place your tab, then press TAB.

3 Repeat step 2 on the following text line. And so on, until all your text is aligned.

...cont'd

Changing tab alignment

Publisher offers four tab alignment options:

- Left edge
- Right edge
- Centre
- Decimal point

When you highlight text to change existing tabs, if you can't see the markers on the ruler, make sure that you've highlighted only the relevant text. If you highlight an area of text which does not have any tab formatting applied, Publisher does not display any tab markers on the ruler.

You can change the alignment of highlighted text easily: simply click the Tab Alignment button – shown on the opposite page – repeatedly until you see the desired alignment icon shown below:

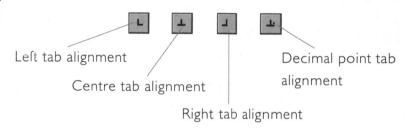

Left tab alignment

Centre tab alignment

Right tab alignment

Decimal point tab alignment

To change the status of tab stops and leaders, you must highlight the text which you want to affect, before choosing a command or starting a procedure.

Moving and removing a tab stop

To move a tab stop marker on the ruler, simply drag the marker to a new position, or off the ruler to delete the tab.

Adding and deleting leaders to tab stops

To help guide the eye, you can add leaders – that is dots, dashes, or lines – to tab stops, as shown opposite. Highlight the text you want to affect and double-click the desired tab stop marker on the ruler. In the Tabs dialog box, under the Leader category, click the leader you want. Then click OK. To delete leaders, highlight the text you want to affect, display the Tabs dialog box again, and click None in the Leaders category. Click OK to confirm your changes.

Deleting all tab stops at the same time

First, highlight the text you want to affect. Then, in the Tabs dialog box, click the Clear All button, followed by the OK button.

Indenting text

When you insert a text indent you affect an entire paragraph (or more if you have highlighted multiple paragraphs). Some examples of indents are shown below:

To quickly delete indents in a high-lighted paragraph, use the Decrease Indent button **on the Formatting toolbar.**

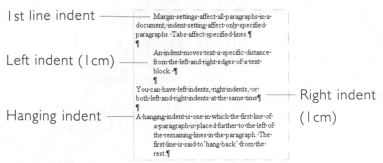

1st line indent

Left indent (1cm)

Hanging indent

Right indent (1cm)

To quickly indent highlighted text, simply click the Increase Indent button **on the Formatting toolbar.**

To create an indent, first highlight the paragraphs you want to indent. Next, click Indents and Lists in the Format menu. Then you can make your choices in the Indents and Lists dialog box as shown below:

1 Click an option in the Preset box: 1st line indent; Hanging indent; Quotation (use step 2 for Custom indents).

2 If you're choosing a Custom indent, click here. Then in the Left, First line, and Right edit boxes, type the desired values.

3 Click OK.

To quickly adjust an indent, first highlight the text containing the indent you want to change. Then, on the ruler, place the mouse pointer on the desired indent marker and simply drag it to the new position.

The ruler showing indent markers for a hanging indent

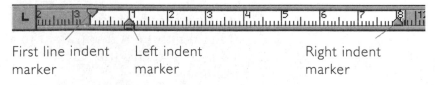

First line indent marker

Left indent marker

Right indent marker

Working with text styles

A defined text style includes formatting attributes that you may apply to any paragraph, and can include font, type size, type style (ie, whether bold, italic, or normal), line spacing, paragraph alignment, tabs, and indents.

Text styles are particularly useful when working on longer documents or documents that are part of a matched set. Using styles in this way, you can keep a consistent look to all related publications from different authors.

While working on publications like newsletters, you could make the job much easier by defining individual styles for the headline, main headings, subheadings, body text, captions and so on.

Once you've defined a style, you can easily apply it to any paragraph in the current document in a single step. To define a new style, apply any of the style formatting attributes listed in the previous paragraphs to reformat the text the way you want. Then, highlight the newly formatted text and perform the following steps:

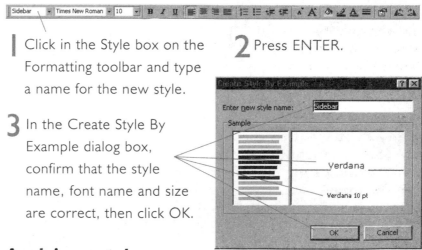

1 Click in the Style box on the Formatting toolbar and type a name for the new style.

2 Press ENTER.

Defining a text style is only the first stage of the process. To use a defined text style, you must apply the style to a paragraph.

3 In the Create Style By Example dialog box, confirm that the style name, font name and size are correct, then click OK.

Enter new style name: Sidebar

Sample

Verdana

Verdana 10 pt

OK   Cancel

Applying a style
To apply a text style to a paragraph, first click in the paragraph to which you want to apply the style. Then, in the Style box on the Formatting toolbar, click the drop-down arrow and click the style you want to apply.

Modifying, deleting and importing styles
Click the Text Style command in the Format menu and Publisher displays the Text Styles dialog box, in which you can create, change, rename, delete and import text styles.

Using Personal Information Sets

Personal information, whether for business or personal use is often used repeatedly in publications. Publisher makes the job of handling repeated personal information easier by using Personal Information Sets.

A Personal Information Set contains basic essential information about you, your business or organisation. A group of components make up a Personal Information Set.

Each Personal Information Set contains the following eight components:

 When you start a new publication, Publisher

- Personal name

- Personal job title

- Name of organisation

- Address of organisation

- Organisation's tag line

- Telephone, fax and e-mail numbers

- Organisation's logo

- Colour scheme

automatically selects the Primary Business Personal Information Set. However, you can choose which Set – if any – you want to use for the current publication using the Personal Information command in the Edit menu.

With a Personal Information Set, you need only enter this information once and from then on can choose to use it as is, or modify it 'on the fly'.

Publisher makes available to you four Personal Information Sets. These are: Primary business (default); Secondary business; Other organisation; and Home/family.

Entering and updating personal information data

To enter the data that makes up your Personal Information components, or change the default Personal Information Set, perform the following steps:

Open the Edit menu and choose the Personal Information command.

...cont'd

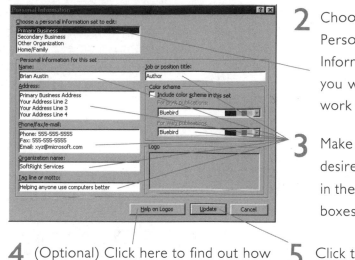

To change information in a Personal Information Set, first make your changes as described here. Finally, save the publication.

2 Choose which Personal Information Set you want to work with.

3 Make your desired changes in the edit boxes.

4 (Optional) Click here to find out how to include your logo.

5 Click the Update button.

If you make a change to one instance of a Personal Information component in a publication, Publisher also changes all other instances of the same type of component to match.

To choose and apply a Personal Information Set to a publication, perform the steps below:

1 Open the Insert menu, choose the Personal Information command followed by the specific Personal Information component you want as shown on the Insert menu below.

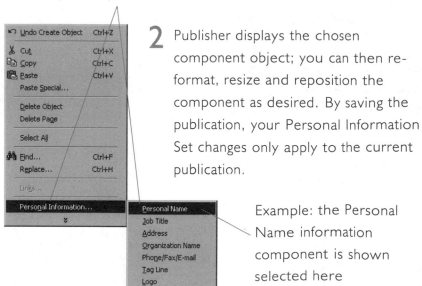

2 Publisher displays the chosen component object; you can then re-format, resize and reposition the component as desired. By saving the publication, your Personal Information Set changes only apply to the current publication.

Example: the Personal Name information component is shown selected here

Using WordArt

The WordArt tool is one of Publisher's most powerful text design assistants. Using the WordArt Frame tool, situated in the Objects toolbar, you can perform a range of special graphic effects to words, like the example shown below. To start WordArt, carry out the steps below:

WordArt is great for trying out ideas and letting your imagination fly. You can twist and turn text, pour words into a shape, apply patterns, colours and shadows, and much more.

1 Click the WordArt Frame tool on the Objects toolbar:

2 Place the mouse pointer where you want the upper left corner of your WordArt frame to be, then drag down diagonally to create the desired frame size.

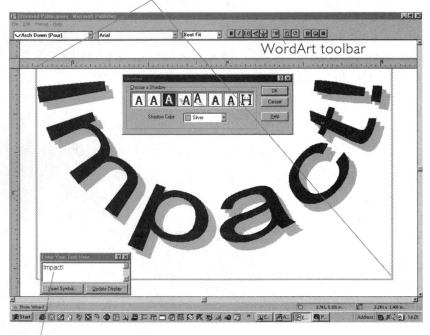

WordArt toolbar

If you decide to use WordArt, print the WordArt page to check that the result is what you expect. WordArt effects can make extra demands on some printers and sometimes text may look fine on the screen but appear too jagged when printed.

3 Type the text to which you want to apply WordArt here. To start a new line, press ENTER.

4 Use the commands and buttons on the WordArt toolbar to apply various effects to your text.

5 Click outside the WordArt frame to exit WordArt.

Creating a fancy first letter

One of the most popular effects to include in a document is to add a fancy first letter – otherwise known as a drop cap – as shown below:

To create a fancy first word, first count the number of letters in the word. Next, perform steps 1 and 3 below. Then, click the Custom Drop Cap tab. Next, in the Number Of Letters box type the number of letters in the first word. Finally, click OK.

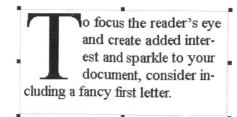

Many people prefer to apply this effect to the first letter in a frame of text. However, you can apply the same technique to an entire word if you wish. Carry out the steps below to create a fancy first letter:

1 With the right mouse button, click the paragraph in which you want to add a fancy first letter.

2 Choose Change Text followed by the Drop Cap command.

To change or remove a fancy first letter, first click in the paragraph containing the letter. Next, click Change Drop Cap in the Format menu. To change the letter, click Custom Drop Cap and make your changes. To remove the letter, click the Remove button. Finally, click OK.

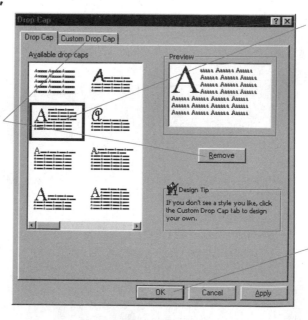

3 In the Drop Cap dialog box, click the fancy letter you want. Use the scroll bar to see more letters.

4 Click OK to create your fancy first letter.

Publisher's non-printing marks

Viewing or hiding Publisher's special characters

As you enter data into your document, Publisher inserts various non-printing special characters. Examples include paragraph marks, which appear every time you press ENTER; tab marks, inserted every time you press the TAB key; and space marks, which appear each time you press the SPACEBAR. Publisher lets you decide if you want to view or hide these and other non-printing characters.

When non-printing characters are displayed, if you want to hide them, simply click the Hide Special Characters command in the View menu. To display the special characters when they are hidden, simply click Show Special Characters in the View menu.

If the document in which you're working contains many varying text and graphic elements, it can be useful periodically to turn off special characters, boundaries and guides to see a clear picture of your document.

When boundaries and guides are turned off, but the Snap To Guides command in the Tools menu is turned on, remember, the snapping action is still active when you move or place objects.

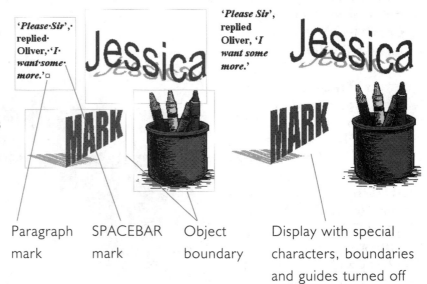

Paragraph mark   SPACEBAR mark   Object boundary   Display with special characters, boundaries and guides turned off

Viewing or hiding boundaries and guides

Publisher also lets you display or hide object boundaries and guides. To hide boundaries and guides, simply click Hide Boundaries And Guides in the View menu. To display boundaries and guides when they are hidden, click Show Boundaries And Guides in the View menu.

Using mail merge

Publisher's mail merge feature shows how all mail merge tools should work. In this chapter, we describe how you can easily print customised address labels for mass mailing. You can also apply the same techniques and print hundreds of customised envelopes or other documents instead.

Covers

Chapter Seven

Setting up your data source

Before you can tap the power of Publisher's mail merge feature, you'll need a mailing list of addresses or other data source, which contains the individual records of information you want to apply to your publication.

Your data source can be created outside of Publisher, in a range of standard word-processor and database formats, like those from Microsoft Word, Access or Excel, dBASE and FoxPro. However, in this example, for a data source, we are going to create a list of addresses in Publisher.

First choose a design from the Label Wizard available in the Catalog dialog box. Once the Wizard is complete, click the text to select it and save time later, then choose the Open Data Source command from the Mail Merge menu. From the following prompt box, click the option to create an address list in Publisher and perform the steps below:

You can also display the New Address List dialog box by clicking the Create Publisher Address List command in the Mail Merge menu.

In the Address List dialog box, Publisher automatically saves the information for each new address when you click the New Entry button.

After creating an address list data source, if you want to edit the list, click the Edit Publisher Address List command in the Mail Merge menu. Then double-click on the list you want to edit.

1 Enter information for the first address in the edit boxes. Press TAB to advance through the edit boxes.

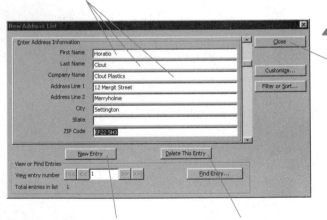

4 After you have entered all the information for every address, click here.

2 Click here to enter details for the following address.

3 (Optional) To delete an entire address record, click here.

5 In the Save As dialog box, type a name in the 'File name' box and click the Save button. Click the Yes button in the following prompt box.

Inserting placeholders

Once you have created your data source as described on the facing page, Publisher displays the Insert Fields dialog box as shown below. This is where you can establish the structure of your address labels.

You can also display the Insert Fields dialog box, by clicking the Insert Field command in the Mail Merge menu.

It's a good idea at this stage to drag the dialog box away from the selected placeholders underneath, if necessary, so that you can see the layout of your work. Then, carry out the steps below to create the address structure you want to use:

1 Click the first field you want to use to select it.

2 Click the Insert button.

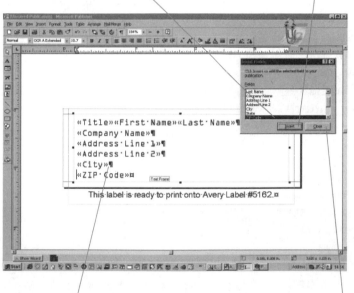

You can format, move and copy placeholders in the same way as ordinary text.

If you make a mistake when inserting a placeholder, you can delete it simply by highlighting the desired placeholder to select it and then pressing the Delete key.

3 Press the Enter key to move the cursor to the next line and include any desired spaces or punctuation marks.

4 Repeat steps 1 to 3 until all placeholders have been inserted, then click Close.

5 Click the Merge command in the Mail Merge menu. Publisher then substitutes the placeholders with the information in the first record of your address list data source.

Checking merged information

After you've chosen the Merge command in the Mail Merge menu, Publisher displays the Preview Data dialog box, as shown below. Publisher also shows the effect of the merged results:

To quickly check if a data source address list has been merged with your publication, first open the Mail Merge menu. If the publication has already been merged, Publisher places a tick mark next to the Merge command.

Click here to step through every address record in your data source, if you want to check the appearance of each label.

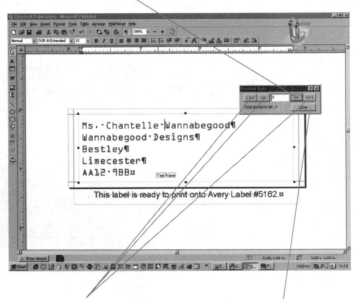

To cancel a merged publication, click the Cancel Merge command in the Mail Merge menu. Publisher prompts you one last time. Click Yes to cancel the merge.

You can use these buttons to navigate through your address list data source

2 Click the Close button when finished.

Viewing a publication's merged data

Once you've merged your data source with a publication and cleared the Preview Data dialog box from the screen, Publisher re-displays the field codes in place of your merged data. However, you can still check your merged data at any time, simply by clicking the Show Merge Results command in the Mail Merge menu.

g a table

Tables are ideal if you want to organize words and numbers in a concise and compact form using rows and columns. Publisher makes the job of creating tables easy, and if you

...provide
...ocal
...int or to
...dd visual
...a table,
...verlay
...ke icons,
...and
...t objects on
...table. Draw
...re frame on
...ble to contain
...mage and
...ly add the
...ge to the frame.
...Chapter 9 for
...re information.

want to provide more sparkle to a table, you can apply various effects like shading, borders, add pictures, and so on, as shown in the example below:

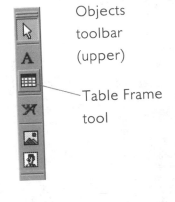

Raspberry sorbet	
Raspberries	500g
Kirsch	1 table spoon
Water	250 ml
Sugar syrup	
Sugar	200 g
water	250 ml

Objects
toolbar
(upper)

Table Frame
tool

The information you put into a table can come from various sources. You can simply start typing in Publisher; copy from existing Publisher text or from another Windows-based application; or you can link or embed a table using OLE (examined on page 47). Now let's look at how to create a table entirely from within Publisher: carry out the steps below and on the facing page:

If you want to add pictures to your table, always establish the size and layout of your table first, then add the pictures. In this way, you make sure the picture enhances the table, not the other way round.

| On the Objects toolbar, click the Table Frame tool.

2 Position the mouse pointer where you want the upper-left corner of your table to appear. Press and hold down the left mouse button while you drag diagonally down to the right, until you see the table size and shape you want, then release the mouse button. It doesn't matter if the table is not exactly the correct size or shape: you can resize it later.

Sorting an address list

Unless you change it, Publisher keeps the original order of your address list. This order is simply the sequence in which you entered your address list data. However, Publisher includes a simple but effective sort tool. This can be useful if, for example, you want to sort your mailing labels so that they print out in ascending postal code order. Alternatively, you may want to sort your address list into alphabetical order to ensure monitoring is easier.

Sorting an address list does not affect the essential information in any way. A sort simply rearranges the order in one of two ways.

To change the order in which the entries in your data source are merged, first click the Filter or Sort command in the Mail Merge menu. Then carry out the steps below:

| Click the Sort tab if necessary.

Sorting will work only if you have merged your publication with a data source and inserted at least one placeholder.

2 Click the field by which you want to sort here.

3 Click either Ascending or Descending sort order.

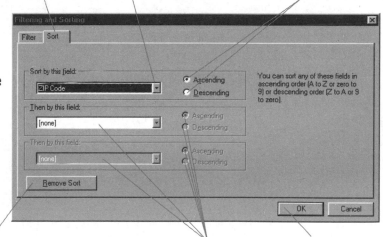

If after changing the sort order you decide that it is not what you want, click the Remove Sort button in the Filtering and Sorting dialog box.

4 (Optional) You can further fine-tune the current sort action by repeating steps 2 to 3 here for the remaining Sort fields.

5 Click the OK button to start the sort.

You can immediately confirm the new sort order before printing, by clicking the Show Merge Results command in the Mail Merge menu and stepping through the addresses in the Preview Data dialog box.

Printing your mail merge

 You change the size of the labels specified using the Labels option from the Page Setup command in the File menu.

 To prevent printing labels for all addresses in your data source, you can apply a filter using the Filter or Sort command in the Mail Merge menu. This can be useful, for example, if you want to print only those addresses from a specific county. See online Help for details.

 Filtering does not affect the addresses in your data source. You can remove a filter by clicking the Remove Filter button in the Filtering and Sorting dialog box.

You're now ready to print your mail merge. Ensure your printer is set up and that the printer tray has the correct sheets of labels installed. Then, click the Print Merge command in the File menu to display the Print Merge dialog box, in which you can specify your options. The following steps illustrate the sequence of events:

1 Click the Page Options button to display the Page Options dialog box and choose the settings your printer manual specifies for the type and size of labels you are using, then click OK (but see step 2 first).

3 Click the Properties button.

4 (Optional) If your printer uses manual feed, click that option.

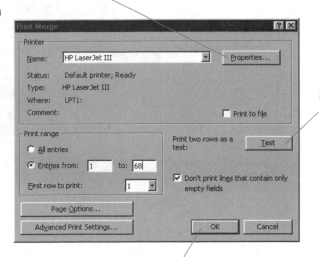

6 Click the Test button to print two rows of labels.

7 If your test printed correctly, click the OK button to print your entire mail merge.

2 (Optional) In the Page Options dialog box, click the Custom Options button to change the margins and space between the labels.

5 Click the OK button till you return to the Print Merge dialog box, and load your printer with label sheets if necessary.

Chapter Eight

Wor...

Tables can help show t...
bring some order and struc...
This chapter explains h...
tables, including adding, dele...
columns. We also look a...
appearance of a table by adding o...

Covers

Creatin...

To... a f... p... a... impact to... you can o... objects i... pictures... WordA... to you... a pictu... the ta... your... simp... ima... See... mo...

3 In the Create Table dialog box, choose the options you want.

To make the job of moving your table and any overlaid objects together easier, you can select the table and all objects on it, and use the Group command in the Arrange menu to group all the table objects together.

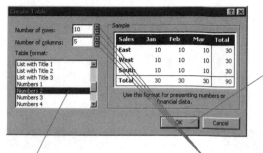

6 Click OK to create your table design.

5 Click a table format from the list available.

4 (Optional) You can change the number of rows and columns by clicking the buttons here.

Table cell boundaries help provide a clear picture. If you can't see cell boundaries, the Hide Boundaries and Guides command is probably switched on. To turn the command off, click Show Boundaries and Guides in the View menu.

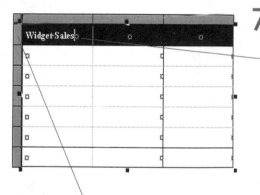

7 Publisher draws your table. Click where you want to start typing and type your entry for the current cell. If your text fills the cell, Publisher automatically expands the cell to contain it.

8 (Optional) In our example above, the first entry is a title. To arrange the title centrally across the top row of the table, first click the left edge of the desired row of the selected table to highlight the row. Then, click the right mouse button over the cell, and click Change Table followed by Merge Cells.

9 To move to the following cell, press TAB. To move to the previous cell, press SHIFT+TAB.

10 Complete your entries for the remaining cells in the table.

Moving around a table

On the previous page, you learnt how to move the insertion point to the following cell, or to the previous cell in a table.

Sometimes, Publisher provides alternative ways in which you can move through a table.

The following illustration, created in table format in Publisher, summarizes the options available to you for moving around a table.

NAVIGATING THROUGH A TABLE IN PUBLISHER	
Destination	**How**
Next cell	Press TAB or RIGHT ARROW key
Previous cell	Press SHIFT+TAB or LEFT ARROW key
Up one cell / line	Press UP ARROW key
Down one cell / line	Press DOWN ARROW key
Any cell	Click in the desired cell
Any existing text in the table	Click the text you want
Next character	Press RIGHT ARROW key
Previous character	Press LEFT ARROW key
Next tab stop in a cell	Press CTRL+TAB

Sorting an address list

Unless you change it, Publisher keeps the original order of your address list. This order is simply the sequence in which you entered your address list data. However, Publisher includes a simple but effective sort tool. This can be useful if, for example, you want to sort your mailing labels so that they print out in ascending postal code order. Alternatively, you may want to sort your address list into alphabetical order to ensure monitoring is easier.

Sorting an address list does not affect the essential information in any way. A sort simply rearranges the order in one of two ways.

To change the order in which the entries in your data source are merged, first click the Filter or Sort command in the Mail Merge menu. Then carry out the steps below:

1 Click the Sort tab if necessary.

Sorting will work only if you have merged your publication with a data source and inserted at least one placeholder.

2 Click the field by which you want to sort here.

3 Click either Ascending or Descending sort order.

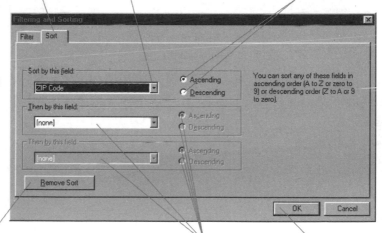

If after changing the sort order you decide that it is not what you want, click the Remove Sort button in the Filtering and Sorting dialog box.

4 (Optional) You can further fine-tune the current sort action by repeating steps 2 to 3 here for the remaining Sort fields.

5 Click the OK button to start the sort.

You can immediately confirm the new sort order before printing, by clicking the Show Merge Results command in the Mail Merge menu and stepping through the addresses in the Preview Data dialog box.

Printing your mail merge

You change the size of the labels specified using the Labels option from the Page Setup command in the File menu.

You're now ready to print your mail merge. Ensure your printer is set up and that the printer tray has the correct sheets of labels installed. Then, click the Print Merge command in the File menu to display the Print Merge dialog box, in which you can specify your options. The following steps illustrate the sequence of events:

1 Click the Page Options button to display the Page Options dialog box and choose the settings your printer manual specifies for the type and size of labels you are using, then click OK (but see step 2 first).

3 Click the Properties button.

4 (Optional) If your printer uses manual feed, click that option.

To prevent printing labels for all addresses in your data source, you can apply a filter using the Filter or Sort command in the Mail Merge menu. This can be useful, for example, if you want to print only those addresses from a specific county. See online Help for details.

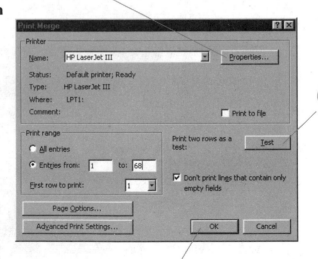

6 Click the Test button to print two rows of labels.

7 If your test printed correctly, click the OK button to print your entire mail merge.

Filtering does not affect the addresses in your data source. You can remove a filter by clicking the Remove Filter button in the Filtering and Sorting dialog box.

2 (Optional) In the Page Options dialog box, click the Custom Options button to change the margins and space between the labels.

5 Click the OK button till you return to the Print Merge dialog box, and load your printer with label sheets if necessary.

Working with tables

Tables can help show the big picture more quickly and bring some order and structure to a mass of information. This chapter explains how you can create and modify tables, including adding, deleting and changing rows and columns. We also look at how you can improve the appearance of a table by adding different types of borders, and pictures.

Chapter Eight

Covers

Creating a table

Tables are ideal if you want to organize words and numbers in a concise and compact form using rows and columns. Publisher makes the job of creating tables easy, and if you want to provide more sparkle to a table, you can apply various effects like shading, borders, add pictures, and so on, as shown in the example below:

 To provide a focal point or to add visual impact to a table, you can overlay objects like icons, pictures and WordArt objects on to your table. Draw a picture frame on the table to contain your image and simply add the image to the frame. See Chapter 9 for more information.

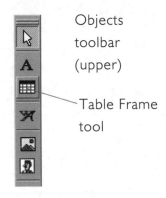

Raspberry sorbet	
Raspberries	500g
Kirsch	1 table spoon
Water	250 ml
Sugar syrup	
Sugar	200 g
water	250 ml

Objects toolbar (upper)

Table Frame tool

If you want to add pictures to your table, always establish the size and layout of your table first, then add the pictures. In this way, you make sure the picture enhances the table, not the other way round.

The information you put into a table can come from various sources. You can simply start typing in Publisher; copy from existing Publisher text or from another Windows-based application; or you can link or embed a table using OLE (examined on page 47). Now let's look at how to create a table entirely from within Publisher: carry out the steps below and on the facing page:

1 On the Objects toolbar, click the Table Frame tool.

2 Position the mouse pointer where you want the upper-left corner of your table to appear. Press and hold down the left mouse button while you drag diagonally down to the right, until you see the table size and shape you want, then release the mouse button. It doesn't matter if the table is not exactly the correct size or shape: you can resize it later.

...cont'd

3 In the Create Table dialog box, choose the options you want.

To make the job of moving your table and any overlaid objects together easier, you can select the table and all objects on it, and use the Group command in the Arrange menu to group all the table objects together.

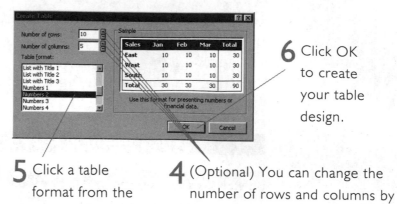

6 Click OK to create your table design.

5 Click a table format from the list available.

4 (Optional) You can change the number of rows and columns by clicking the buttons here.

Table cell boundaries help provide a clear picture. If you can't see cell boundaries, the Hide Boundaries and Guides command is probably switched on. To turn the command off, click Show Boundaries and Guides in the View menu.

7 Publisher draws your table. Click where you want to start typing and type your entry for the current cell. If your text fills the cell, Publisher automatically expands the cell to contain it.

8 (Optional) In our example above, the first entry is a title. To arrange the title centrally across the top row of the table, first click the left edge of the desired row of the selected table to highlight the row. Then, click the right mouse button over the cell, and click Change Table followed by Merge Cells.

9 To move to the following cell, press TAB. To move to the previous cell, press SHIFT+TAB.

10 Complete your entries for the remaining cells in the table.

Moving around a table

On the previous page, you learnt how to move the insertion point to the following cell, or to the previous cell in a table.

Sometimes, Publisher provides alternative ways in which you can move through a table.

The following illustration, created in table format in Publisher, summarizes the options available to you for moving around a table.

NAVIGATING THROUGH A TABLE IN PUBLISHER	
Destination	**How**
Next cell	Press TAB or RIGHT ARROW key
Previous cell	Press SHIFT+TAB or LEFT ARROW key
Up one cell / line	Press UP ARROW key
Down one cell / line	Press DOWN ARROW key
Any cell	Click in the desired cell
Any existing text in the table	Click the text you want
Next character	Press RIGHT ARROW key
Previous character	Press LEFT ARROW key
Next tab stop in a cell	Press CTRL+TAB

Selecting in tables

To recap, whenever you want to change or modify something in Publisher, you must select what you want to affect, before choosing the commands to bring about the desired change. This is also true when working with tables in Publisher, with some variations on what you might expect.

The table below summarizes how to select any part of a table in Publisher. The options covering row and column selection and entire table selection relate to the diagram following the table.

 To select multiple rows or columns, as you select the first row or column in the chain, make sure you place the mouse pointer in the middle of a row or column Selector marker before drag-selecting over the remaining row or column markers. Otherwise, you may resize rows or columns.

 You can easily identify the middle of a row or column Selector marker. When you place the mouse pointer on it, Publisher changes the mouse pointer symbol to a hand pointer icon.

TABLE SELECTING OPTIONS IN PUBLISHER	
Selection target	**How**
Some text in a cell	Drag insertion point across the text
A single word	Double-click the desired word
All text in a cell	Click desired cell, then press CTRL+A
Text in adjacent cells	Click where you want the highlight to start, hold down SHIFT, then click where you want highlight to end
A specified cell	Drag-select over the desired cell
Any number of neighbouring cells	Drag-select over the desired cells
A single row or coloumn	Click the table to select it, then click the desired Selector marker shown below (R=row, C=column)
Several rows or columns	Drag-select across desired row or column Selector markers shown below (R=row, C=column)
Entire table	Click the table to select it, then click the Entire Table Selector button

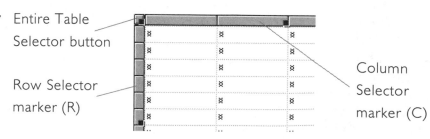

Entire Table Selector button

Row Selector marker (R)

Column Selector marker (C)

Changing row and column size

To quickly resize a row or column without changing the overall size of a table, hold down the SHIFT key while you drag the row or column Adjust symbol.

Sometimes, as you add and modify cell contents in a table, rows and columns may need to be resized to display cell contents clearly and neatly. To resize a row or column, perform the steps below:

1 If the table is not already selected, click it.

2 Position the mouse pointer on the boundary of the row or column you want to change until you see the Adjust symbol appear.

To resize two or more rows or columns at the same time, first highlight all the rows or columns you want to resize. Then, adjust the rows or columns as if you're adjusting a single row or column.

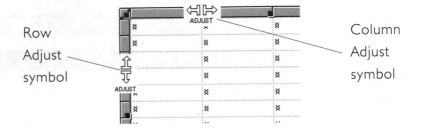

Row Adjust symbol

Column Adjust symbol

3 With the appropriate Adjust symbol visible, hold down the left mouse button and drag the row or column boundary to display the new row or column width, then release the mouse button.

You can change how text looks in a table in the same way you change text in Publisher generally – ie, highlight the text you want to change, then click the desired button on the Formatting toolbar.

Resizing an entire table

The task of resizing an entire table is made easier by the fact that Publisher considers a table to be an object. Remember, in Chapters 2 and 3, we examined the properties of objects. Therefore, to resize a table, first simply click the table to select it. Next, place the mouse pointer over one of the Selection handles until you see the Resize symbol. Then, hold down the left mouse button and drag the mouse to display the table size you want. Finally, release the mouse button.

When you resize a table in this way, the proportions of all cells are affected to the same extent.

Adding rows and columns

After you've created your basic table, you may want to insert more rows or columns. You can do this using the Insert Rows or Columns command in the Table menu, or by using the floating menu which Publisher displays when you press the right mouse button. To insert rows or columns, carry out the steps below:

1 With the left mouse button, click the row or column next to where you want to insert a new row or column.

2 With the mouse pointer placed on the table, click the right mouse button to display the floating menu.

To quickly add a row at the bottom of a table, click in the lower-most right cell in the table and press the TAB key.

3 Click the Change Table command followed by Insert Rows or Columns command.

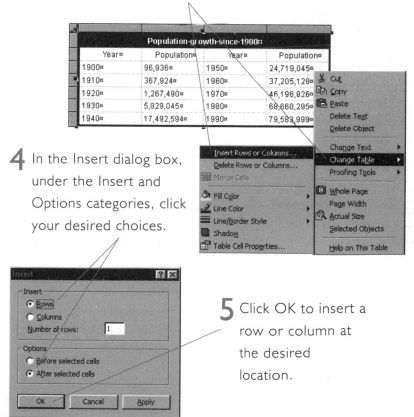

4 In the Insert dialog box, under the Insert and Options categories, click your desired choices.

5 Click OK to insert a row or column at the desired location.

Moving and copying cell data

After developing a table, you may decide you want to move the contents of some cells, either to somewhere else within the same table, to another Publisher table, or even to another compatible Windows-based application. To move and copy information, Publisher provides the Cut, Copy and Paste commands in the Edit menu: commands which are also accessible when clicking the right mouse button. To move cell data, carry out the steps below:

 To quickly move a cell's text to another location, first highlight the cell containing the text you want to move. Next, place the mouse pointer over the highlighted cells until you see the Drag symbol. Then hold down the left mouse button and drag the highlighted text to the new location. Then release the mouse button.

1 If you want to move or copy cell data to another table in another Publisher document, start another session of Publisher and open the document to which you want to move the cell data. This is the target document.

2 Back in the source document, highlight the table cells containing the information you want to move or copy.

3 With the mouse pointer placed on top of the cells you want to move or copy, click the right mouse button.

4 On the floating menu, click the Cut command to move data or the Copy command to copy data.

5 In the destination table, if you want to replace existing cells, highlight the cells to which you want to move or copy data. But if you want to move or copy to new empty cells, click the cell in which you want the upper-left corner of the cut text to be placed.

6 Click the right mouse button.

7 On the floating menu, click Paste.

Deleting rows and columns

You can easily delete rows or columns using the Delete Rows, Delete Columns, or Delete Rows or Columns commands in the Table menu. However, arguably, it's easier to use the right mouse button. To delete a row or column, carry out the steps below:

Highlight the row(s) or column(s) you want to delete.

To delete some but not all text in a table, simply highlight all the text you want to delete, then press the DELETE key.

Click here to highlight a column

Population growth since1890			
Year	Population	Year	Population
1890	96,936	1940	24,719,045
1900	367,924	1950	37,459,207
1910	1,267,490	1960	46,278,229
1920	5,829,045	1970	68,346,255
1930	17,492,594	1980	79,334,527

To quickly delete an entire table, with the right mouse button, click the table you want to delete. Then from the floating menu, click the Delete Object command.

Population growth since1890		Select Table Column	
Year	Population	Year	Population
1890	96,936	1940	24,719,045
1900	367,924	1950	37,459,207
1910	1,267,490	1960	46,278,229
1920	5,829,045	1970	68,346,255
1930	17,492,594	1980	79,334,527

Click here to highlight a row

2 With the right mouse button, click the highlighted row or column.

3 On the floating menu, click the Change Table command, then click either the Delete Rows or Delete Columns command.

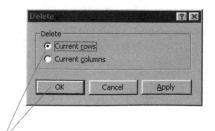

If you don't highlight a full row or column before clicking the right mouse button, Publisher makes available the Delete Rows or Columns command on the menus. If you then click this command, in the Delete dialog box, you can decide whether to delete the row or column containing the current selection.

Changing how cell data looks

There are several ways in which you can enhance the appearance of a table and make it more attractive and clearer to see. You can use crisp, clear fonts and apply colours – if appropriate. Table titles and subheadings can be easily identified at a glance when comprised of light-coloured text on a dark background. Also, subtle shading helps provide a medium level of importance in a hierarchy of headings, as shown in the example below. To apply shading to a table, perform the following steps:

Population·growth·since·1900			
Year¤	Population¤	Year¤	Population¤
1900¤	96,936¤	1950¤	24,719,045¤
1910¤	367,924¤	1960¤	37,205,128¤
1920¤	1,267,490¤	1970¤	46,196,826¤
1930¤	5,829,045¤	1980¤	68,668,295¤
1940¤	17,492,594¤	1990¤	79,583,999¤

Sometimes shading can interfere with the clarity of a table. Therefore, if using lighter, smaller sized fonts, you may consider shading is not a worthwhile option.

1 Highlight all the cells to which you want to apply shading.

2 On the Formatting toolbar, click the Fill Color button.

3 On the Colors palette, click the Fill Effects button.

Font Color button

4 In the Fill Effects dialog box, click the shading options you want.

5 Click OK to apply the chosen shading to the highlighted areas of your table.

To change the colour of a table border, first click the table to select it. If you want to affect a specific part of a table border, highlight the cells next to the part of the border you want to change. Then, on the Formatting toolbar, click the Line/Border Style button, followed by the More Styles command. Under the Color category, click a new colour, followed by OK.

Changing the colour of objects

Here's another way to change the colour of a table border quickly. First, click the table to select it, then highlight the entire table by clicking the Select (all) Cells button situated at the uppermost left corner. Next, click the table with the right mouse button and choose the Change Table command, followed by Line/Border Style then More Styles. In the Border/Style dialog box with the Line Border tab contents displayed, choose the new desired colour.

You can easily change the colour of cells, rows and columns, cell text, and table borders, in addition to changing or adding shading and patterns to cells. To change text colour, follow the procedures below:

I Click the table to select it.

2 Highlight the desired cells.

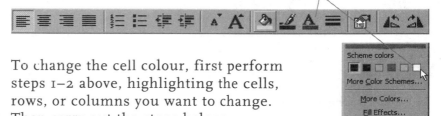

| Population growth since 1890 | | | |
Year	Population	Year	Population
1890	96,936	1940	24,719,045
1900	367,924	1950	37,459,207
1910	1,267,490	1960	46,278,229
1920	5,829,045	1970	68,346,255
1930	17,492,594	1980	79,334,527

3 Click the Font Color button on the Formatting toolbar, then click the desired colour on the floating palette.

To change the cell colour, first perform steps 1–2 above, highlighting the cells, rows, or columns you want to change. Then carry out the steps below:

I On the Formatting toolbar, click the Fill Color button.

2 On the floating palette, click the colour you want.

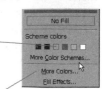

3 (Optional) To see more colours, click the More Colours button. Then click the colour you want, followed by clicking the OK button.

Merging and unmerging cells

As you develop a table, sometimes you may want to merge several cells in a specific row. For example, we often merge cells when inserting a table title or subtitle as shown in the illustrations on these pages. Cells that you choose to merge must all be in the same row. To merge cells, perform the procedure below:

When you merge cells, you don't have to merge an entire row – just two or more highlighted cells are enough to make the Merge Cells command available.

1 If the table is not already selected, click it.

2 Highlight the cells you want to merge.

3 With the right mouse button, click the highlighted cells.

4 Click the Change Table command followed by the Merge Cells command.

If the cells you choose to merge contain text, Publisher forms each piece of text into a separate paragraph in the merged cell. If you're not happy with the result, immediately click the Undo button on the Standard toolbar and re-plan your table.

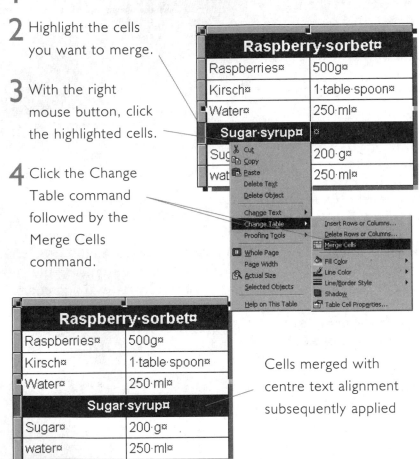

Cells merged with centre text alignment subsequently applied

If you change your mind, you can quickly unmerge cells by first performing steps 1–3 above. Then, on the floating menu, click the Split Cells command which takes the place of the Merge Cells command.

Adding an object to a table

To provide a focal point or to add greater visual impact to a table, you can add objects like icons, pictures, and WordArt objects. However, if you add objects to a table in this way, they do not become part of the table in the same way as a table cell. Rather, a picture is overlaid onto a cell or several cells as shown in the illustration below. To include a picture or other object in a table, carry out the following steps:

 If you want to add pictures to your table, always establish the size and layout of your table first, then add the pictures. In this way, you can ensure a picture matches appropriately to a table, not the other way round.

1 On the Objects toolbar, click the tool you want to use to create a frame for the object you want.

2 Draw a frame on top of the table cell or cells which you want to contain your picture or other object.

3 Place the picture or object onto the frame. Pictures can be inserted using the Picture and Object commands available from the Insert menu. Apply a WordArt object using the procedures described in Chapter 6, page 88.

 To make the job of moving your table, and any overlaid objects together easier, you can select the table and all objects on it, and use the Group Objects command in the Arrange menu to group all selected objects together. Alternatively, click the Group Objects button (see page 41).

Raspberry sorbet	
Raspberries	500g
Kirsch	1 table spoon
Water	250 ml
Sugar syrup	
Sugar	200 g
water	250 ml

Here, an appropriately chosen picture is placed to enhance the table, creating a compelling presentation

You may need to resize and move your object to display the object in the desired position. Remember, you can use Publisher's layout guides, zoom commands and the SHIFT key to help accurately resize and align an object.

Applying cell and table borders

Normally, when you create a table, Publisher inserts cell boundaries around each cell. As explained at the beginning of this chapter, these cell boundaries may be visible. If they're hidden, you can make them visible by clicking the Show Boundaries and Guides command in the View menu.

However, cell boundary lines don't print out: they simply show where one cell ends and another begins. To apply a cell border to each cell, carry out the following steps:

1 Highlight the entire table or only the cells to which you want to apply grid lines.

2 Click the right mouse button over the highlighted cells.

 If you want to spice up a table, consider adding a fancy border. With the Border Style dialog box displayed, click the BorderArt tab to see the range available.

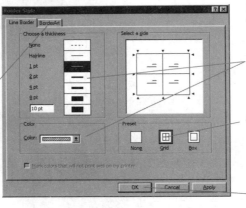

5 (Optional) You can choose a different grid line thickness and colour if you wish.

4 In the Border Style dialog, under the Preset category, click Grid.

6 Click OK.

3 Click the Change Table command followed by the Line/Border Style and More Styles commands.

Adding a table border

To add or change a border around an entire table, first highlight the cell(s) around which you want to place a border. Next, on the Formatting toolbar, click the Line/ Border Style button. You can then simply click a border on the fly-out menu or click the More Styles command to display the Border Style dialog box as shown above. Click a border and optionally click another colour. Finally, click OK to finish.

Chapter Nine

Working with pictures

Sometimes pictures can tell us most of what we need to know about a topic at a glance. In this chapter, we explore how to insert, move and manipulate pictures in a publication. You can also learn how to apply clip art pictures and photographs from the Publisher Clip Gallery to further enhance your documents.

Covers

Placing a picture on the page

 Bitmap pictures are made up of a series of aligned dots. To avoid creating a jagged effect, try not to stretch or enlarge a bitmapped picture.

 Vector-based pictures, keep their original quality when you stretch or scale them.

 To see the range of picture formats Publisher can import, click Picture in the Insert menu, followed by From File. Then click the Files of type arrow button.

 If you're going to be working with pictures regularly, it's worth spending some time learning about the different formats available.

Pictures provide a focal point to a page that text can never equal. Publisher comes with over 10,000 pieces of clip art, 1500 photos and 300 animated pictures stored in the Clip Gallery. And you can also download more images from a special page on the Microsoft Web site.

Clip art pictures for use in desktop publishing come in a range of different file types. However, all clip art can be grouped into two categories: bitmapped or vector. Bitmapped pictures include clip art with the filename extensions of .BMP, .JPG and .TIF; whereas common vector-based clip art filename extensions include: .EPS, .WMF, and .CGM.

To place a clip art picture on your page, first draw a new frame by clicking the Clip Gallery tool 🖾 on the Objects toolbar and then dragging a rectangle shape on the page. As soon as you release the mouse button, Publisher displays the Insert Clip Art dialog box. Then carry out the steps below:

1 Click the Pictures tab.

2 Click the Picture Category containing the type of pictures you want.

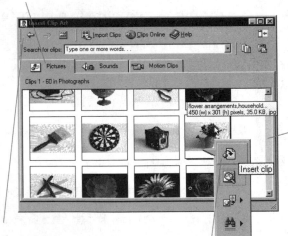

3 (Optional) Use the scroll bar to see more categories and pictures.

4 (Optional) Use the Back button to return to the 'index' of categories at any time.

5 Click the image you want. From the flyout, click the Insert clip button.

Resizing a picture

 Remember, you can resize several pictures at the same time by grouping the pictures you want to resize, as described in *Grouping and ungrouping objects* in Chapter 3.

As you place text and graphic objects on your page, often you may adjust the individual elements to achieve the desired balance. To resize a picture, you can carry out the procedures in *Resizing objects* in Chapter 3. However, sometimes you may want to resize a picture more precisely.

To adjust the size of a picture in defined increments, carry out the steps below:

1 Click the picture to select it.

2 Click the Scale Picture command in the Format menu.

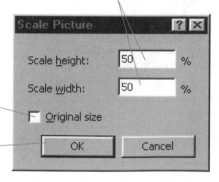

 If you want to place a picture that isn't part of Publisher's Clip Gallery, first draw a picture frame using the Picture Frame Tool on the Objects toolbar (see illustration below). Then use the Picture command and the From File command on the Insert menu to find the picture you want:

3 In the Scale Picture dialog box, type the percentage you want in the Scale height and/or Scale width edit boxes.

Click here to restore original picture size

4 Click OK to make your changes.

If, after resizing a picture, you change your mind, click the Undo button immediately.

If you try several resize cycles but then decide you want to restore the original picture dimensions, first display the Scale Picture dialog box as described above. Next, click the Original size check box, followed by the OK button.

Cropping a picture

Sometimes, you may not want to use an entire picture, just a part of it. You can manipulate a picture to hide the part you don't want or reveal only the part you do want. In Publisher, this is called cropping.

Remember, when you crop a picture, you're not actually deleting the part you crop, but simply hiding what you don't want to appear in print. If you change your mind later, you can easily uncrop the picture to restore the original image. To crop a picture, first click the picture you want to crop. Then, carry out the following steps:

To crop more than one side of a picture at the same time, simply hold down the CTRL key as you crop – ie, to crop all sides equally, crop on a corner selection handle; to crop opposite sides equally, crop on a side handle.

1 On the Formatting toolbar, click the Crop Picture button.

2 Place the mouse pointer over a frame selection handle until the mouse pointer changes to the Crop symbol.

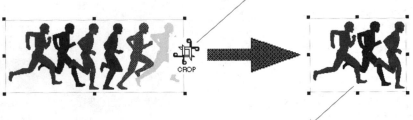

3 Drag the mouse pointer in the desired direction until you've cropped the picture sufficiently. You may need to zoom in further to maintain greater precision.

4 When finished, click the Crop Picture button again to switch it off.

To uncrop a picture, first click the desired picture. Next, click the Crop Picture button. Then, reverse the drag action performed earlier to reveal the entire picture again. Lastly, click the Crop Picture button to turn it off.

Changing the colours in a picture

After placing a picture on the page, you may be able to change all the colours in the picture to different shades of a single colour (not with EPS images though). One situation in which this requirement might be valuable is when you want to create a watermark effect, like the illustration shown below, and then place the image on the background of your publication (the background is examined in Chapter 2). To perform this action, carry out the steps below:

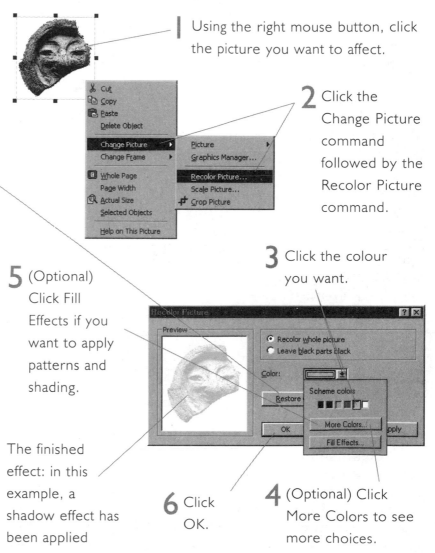

If you don't like the colour change, you can quickly reverse the action. With the picture selected and the Recolor dialog box displayed, click the Restore Original Colors button.

1 Using the right mouse button, click the picture you want to affect.

2 Click the Change Picture command followed by the Recolor Picture command.

3 Click the colour you want.

5 (Optional) Click Fill Effects if you want to apply patterns and shading.

The finished effect: in this example, a shadow effect has been applied

6 Click OK.

4 (Optional) Click More Colors to see more choices.

Moving a picture

You may be able to move an object to another Windows application. To try this, with the right mouse button, click the object you want to move, followed by the Cut command. Next, move to your destination application, then click Paste in its Edit menu.

The Clipboard is a temporary storage area that is part of the Windows standard. You use it, when you carry out cut, copy and paste operations.

You can use Ruler Guides and the 'Snap to ...' commands to help position a picture precisely. See Chapter 3 for more information.

Designing a publication exactly the way you want it can sometimes involve much trial and error – not least with the placement of pictures. Fortunately in Publisher, moving a picture is a simple job, and you have several options. You can place a picture:

- Somewhere else on the same page.

- On another page in the current document.

- On the non-printing workspace area while you decide where you want to put it.

- In another Publisher document.

- In another compatible Windows application.

Moving objects is discussed in Chapter 3. However, if you want to move a picture to another page, arguably the easiest way is simply to drag the object onto the non-printing workspace area (shown below). Next, move to the page on which you want to place your picture, and then simply drag it into position on that page.

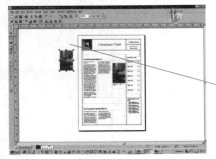

Non-printing workspace area – an ideal temporary storage area

Moving a picture using the Clipboard

First, right-click on the picture you want to move, then click the Cut command. Next, move to or open the publication to which you want to move the picture and display the page you want. With the right mouse button, click anywhere on the workspace. Then choose the Paste command. Finally, drag your picture to the exact location on the page.

Copying a picture

You can copy a picture using the Copy and Paste commands, which may be available on the Edit menu and when you click the right mouse button to select the picture you want to copy.

When you copy a picture, Publisher places an identical image of your picture on to the Windows Clipboard (see previous page for more information about the Windows Clipboard).

To quickly make a copy or multiple copies of a picture, first click the picture to select it. Next, place the mouse pointer on the picture edge until you see the mouse pointer change to the Mover symbol. Then hold down the CTRL key while you drag the mouse where you want your copy to be placed and release the mouse button.

When you use the Paste command, Publisher takes a copy of the object placed on the Clipboard and places it on the page or workspace at the location you specify.

Once a picture (or any other object) is copied to the Clipboard, you can take as many copies as you wish with the Paste command. To copy a picture, perform the following steps:

1 Using the right mouse button, click the picture or graphic object you want to copy.

2 Click the Copy command.

3 Move to where you want to place the copied picture.

4 Using the right mouse button, click where you want to place your picture or graphic object.

5 From the menu that appears, click the Paste command.

Deleting a picture

On pages 116/7, we examined how a picture can be moved to the Windows Clipboard using the Cut command. Then, if you change your mind, you can retrieve the Cut picture – simply click the Undo button immediately. If you carry out further mouse or menu actions, you may not be able to use Undo to retrieve the cut picture, although Publisher 2000 can undo up to 20 actions in sequence. Also, you may still be able to retrieve your cut picture using the Paste command.

If you really want to delete a picture, here's how. Follow the steps below:

To delete several pictures at the same time, hold down SHIFT while you click each picture you want to delete. Then press the DELETE key.

If you change your mind or delete the wrong picture by mistake, immediately click the Undo button after deleting your picture, to have Publisher restore your picture.

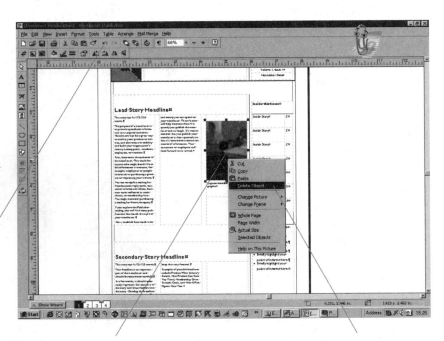

1 Using the right mouse button, click the picture you want to delete.

2 Click the Delete Object command.

Alternatively, click the picture you want to delete, then press the DELETE key. Again, if you change your mind, click the Undo button, Undo command from the Edit menu, or simply close the publication without saving. Your picture will be present next time you open the publication.

Changing the screen redraw speed

The size and complexity of a picture (especially photographic images), and the speed with which your computer processes complex images, affect how quickly your PC draws an image on the screen. If you find images are taking too long to redraw when you zoom or move from page to page, you can reduce the resolution or even hide the images entirely, leaving picture placeholders where your pictures would normally appear while working on the general layout of your document.

If you've reduced the picture display resolution, but later want to re-display it at full resolution, first click the Picture Display command in the View menu. Next, click Detailed Display, followed by OK.

If you reduce the resolution of your picture display, or hide a picture as described below, when you print, your printer can still print pictures using its full resolution. To change your picture display resolution, first click the Picture Display command in the View menu. Then carry out the steps below:

To speed up the picture redraw speed of Publisher-based images, click Fast Resize and Zoom.

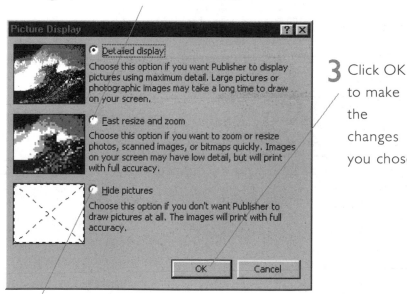

3 Click OK to make the changes you chose.

2 (Optional) Alternatively, to have Publisher hide pictures and replace each one with an X simply as a placement reference, click Hide Pictures.

Using the Clip Gallery

The Clip Gallery can store all your clip art in one place, and make the job of finding, previewing and placing a specific picture on the page easy. You access the Clip Gallery when you click the Picture command followed by Clip Art command on the Insert menu.

If you no longer want to keep specific images in the Gallery, you can delete them. If you do this, remember, you're not actually deleting them from your hard disk, only from the Gallery (see page 122).

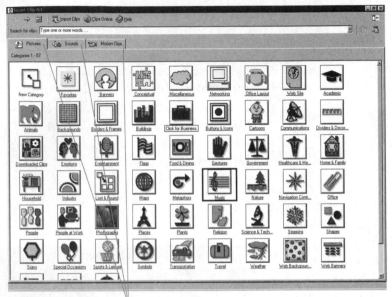

If you have a scanner connected to your PC, you can place a scanned image directly into your publication. Use the From Scanner Or Camera command in the Insert > Picture menu, followed by the Acquire Image command. Use the Select Device command to set which scan software you want to use.

Clip art created in other applications can also be stored in the Clip Gallery, including sound and video files. You can create new Categories and modify the descriptions of existing Categories. However, sometimes Publisher won't store a picture in the Gallery. This can result from any of the following causes:

- The picture format is not compatible with Publisher.

- The filename extension is incorrect. For example, if you know the image is a .CGM file, but it has a different extension, try renaming the file using the correct filename extension.

- The picture file may be damaged. Try reinstalling the original file. Then try to store the image in the Gallery again.

Adding a picture to the Gallery

You can easily see the range of file formats which Publisher can import. Just click the arrow button on the right of the 'Files of type' box in the 'Add clip to Clip Gallery' dialog box.

It's easy to import several picture files at the same time. In the 'Add clip to Clip Gallery' dialog box, simply press and hold down the CTRL key as you click the files you want.

To create a new category for your clip, with the Clip Properties dialog box displayed, click the New Category button, type a new category name and click OK.

To add a picture to the Gallery, carry out the following steps. Repeat steps 2–6 for each picture you want to add:

1 On the Insert menu, click the Picture command followed by the Clip Art command.

2 In the Insert Clip Art dialog box, click the Import Clips button.

3 Click the down arrow button to locate the clip you want.

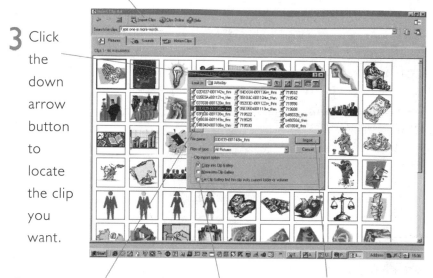

4 Highlight each clip you want: you can import multiple clips in a single action.

6 Click the Import button.

5 Choose the import option you want: (a) Copy it to the Clip gallery; (b) Move the clip to the Clip Gallery, or (c) Leave the clip where it is and simply point to its existing location (ideal when working with CD-ROMs and computer networks).

6 Enter the following details about each clip: description, categories and keywords in the Clip Properties dialog box. Click OK to confirm your entries.

Deleting a picture from the Gallery

To delete a picture from the Clip Gallery, but not from your hard disk, perform the following steps:

1 On the Insert menu, click Picture followed by Clip Art to display the Insert Clip Art dialog box.

2 Click the Category picture representing the Category containing the clip you want to delete.

Pictures deleted from the Gallery are still present on your hard disk. However, deleted picture categories are no longer available to you.

You can use the Search tool to quickly locate the picture file you want to delete. Choose your desired options, click the image and press the DELETE key.

4 Publisher asks you to confirm; click OK to finish.

3 Using the right mouse button, click the clip you want to delete and choose the Delete command.

After you delete a picture from the Gallery, Publisher also removes the preview image from the viewer.

Deleting picture Categories

To delete an entire picture category, Insert Clip Art dialog box, with the 'top level' Categories displayed, with the right mouse button, click the Category you want to delete. Then, from the floating menu, click the Delete Category command. Publisher asks you to confirm that this is what you want to do; click OK. Note: any clips in the Category to delete remain un-deleted.

Chapter Ten

Considering page design

How your pages look makes a difference. This chapter focuses on how Publisher can help you achieve the effect you want. We explore the Design Gallery and take a closer look at the BorderArt Gallery. We also delve into some of the most eye-catching design aspects – logos, mastheads, and the technique of wrapping text around a picture.

Covers

A brochure – an example PageWizard

In Chapter 1, we introduced PageWizards. As PageWizards include many page design aspects for you, on this page, we're going to take a closer look at a Brochure PageWizard. Remember, you can display the Catalog dialog box either when you start Publisher or by choosing the New command in the File menu. With the Catalog dialog box displayed, perform the steps below:

This example Brochure template has two sides. Page 1 is the brochure outside, page 2 the inside. When you print, the two pages can be printed or copied onto both sides of a single sheet of paper.

You can change your mind about the design at any stage. Simply click the component here to re-examine and try out different options displayed in the lower box.

Click a text frame to start entering text and double-click each graphic you want to change.

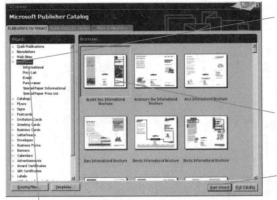

1 Click here to show the range of brochure Wizards available.

3 Click the brochure you want.

4 Click the Start Wizard button.

2 Click the brochure type you want.

6 Click here to hide (or show) the Wizard.

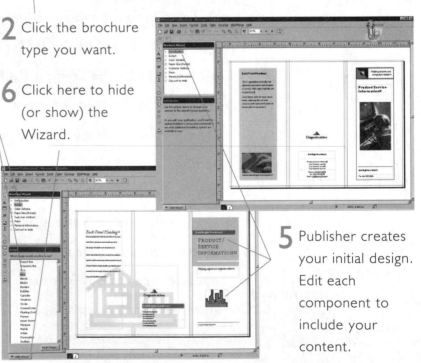

5 Publisher creates your initial design. Edit each component to include your content.

Opening the Design Gallery

The Design Gallery is an excellent collection of predesigned objects which you can include in your publications. The text and graphic objects typically include: headline and masthead designs, pull-quotes, forms, table of contents designs, logos, advertisements and calendars.

 The Design Gallery provides an excellent platform on which you can combine your own ideas and try different combinations to see which produces the results you're looking for.

Many of the objects are designed to match the styles used in Publisher's PageWizards. For example, if you used the Brochure PageWizard, the Design Gallery can offer alternatives by matching components to include with or instead of objects already placed.

You can also store design elements which you create in the Design Gallery, allowing you to access them easily again and again. Publisher also makes the job of finding your design elements easy by grouping related objects into categories. If you can't find the right category in which to store an object, simply create a new category to suit your needs.

 By default, the Design Gallery contains objects that are relevant to the type of publication you're working on. For example, if you're creating a Web page, you'll find Web page objects available, but if you're working on a print-based publication, Web page Objects won't be available.

To open the Design Gallery, simply click the Design Gallery Object button on the Objects toolbar. Publisher then displays the opening Design Gallery dialog box, as shown below:

Design Gallery Object button:

Design Gallery Mastheads library

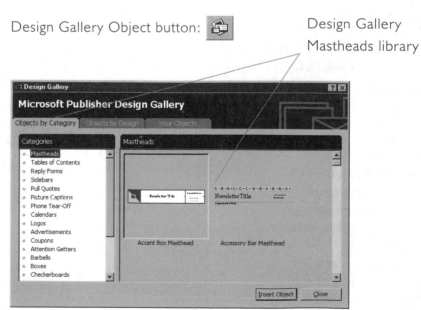

Choosing a Design Gallery object

Sometimes more designs are available than can be seen. Use the scroll buttons to see the hidden designs if they're available.

To add an object from the Design Gallery to your publication, first click the Design Gallery Object button on the Objects toolbar, then carry out the steps below:

1 Click the tab you want: you can view objects by Category, by Design, or Your own Objects (examined later).

3 Click the object you want to select it.

Double-click here to quickly place your object on the page.

To import a Design Gallery object, first, click the Design Gallery Object button on the Objects toolbar. Next, click the Your Objects tab. Click Options, followed by the Browse button. Click the name of the document containing the Design Gallery object you want, then click OK. Click the desired Category, then double-click the desired object.

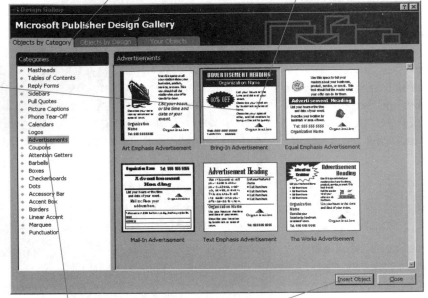

2 Click the Category you want.

4 Click the Insert Object button.

5 Publisher places your chosen object on the page.

g Design Gallery Categories

You can create a new Category and add it to the design set of the current publication. On this page, we're going to look at how to add a new Category to the current document. Carry out the steps below to do this:

1 Click the Design Gallery Object button on the Objects toolbar:

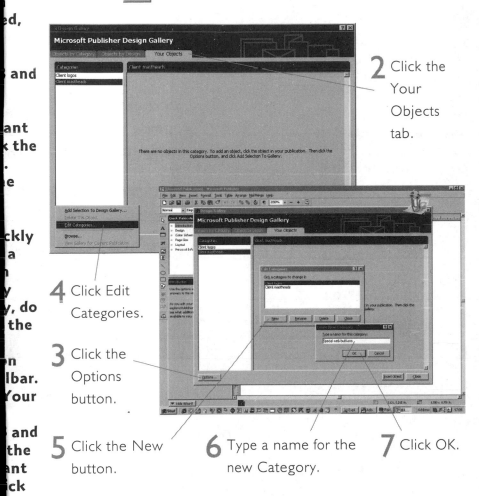

2 Click the Your Objects tab.

4 Click Edit Categories.

3 Click the Options button.

5 Click the New button.

6 Type a name for the new Category.

7 Click OK.

Publisher only records the changes you've made to the Design Gallery when you save the current publication. Therefore, it's a good idea to save immediately after making any important changes here.

Changing a Design Gallery object

After you've placed a Design Gallery object, you can still experiment with different designs. Here's how:

1 On the object, click the 'Wizard: Click to start' button.

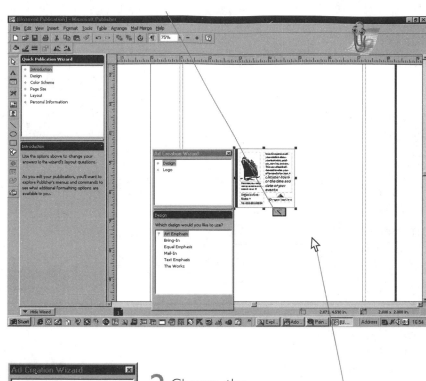

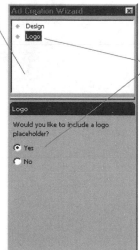

Sometimes, only one pane is displayed. This is normal; the results depend on your choices.

2 Choose the options you want: click an option in the top pane, then answer the questions displayed in the lower pane.

3 To close the Wizard, simply click any empty space on the page or workspace.

Adding objects to the Design Gallery

With every new publication, Publisher creates an empty design set. You can add design elements to the current document design set, to the design sets that come with Publisher, or to objects from other compatible documents. On this page, we're going to add objects to the current document design set. To do this, perform the steps below:

1 Click the design element you want to add to the current design set.

Pyramid·Training

Objects you add to the Design Gallery are not, by default, available to any other Publisher documents. However, you can import them at any time (see the lower DON'T FORGET icon on page 126).

2 Click the Add Selection To Design Gallery command on the Insert menu.

3 Type here a name for the object you're adding.

4 Click the Category you want from the drop-down list or type a new Category name here.

5 Click OK to add the object to the desired Category.

6 Save the current publication. Any objects you add to the Design Gallery for this publication are then saved as part of the publication's design set.

Deleting Design Ga

You can delete obje
listed under the You
currently working o
Publisher's own De
available from the (
Design tabs.

To delete a Design (

After you've deleted a Design Gallery object, it's not really deleted until you save the current publication.

If you delete an object by mistake, simply close the current publication without saving it, then reopen the publication – the 'deleted' object will still be available.

1 Click the Design (
toolbar:

3 Under the Catego
the Category con
object you want t

4 In the right pane, click the object you want to delete to select it.

Creatin

To rer a Desi Galler Categ with the Design Gallery display click the Your Objects tab. Perform steps 4 below and highlight the Category you w to rename. Clic Rename button Type a new nan and click OK.

To qui delete Desig Galler Object Categor this. First, click Design Gallery Object button c the Objects too Next, click the Objects tab. Perform steps 4 and highlight category you w to delete and c the Close butto

Creating a logo

Logos are everywhere! We see symbols of all kinds all the time. But to create the right look and put over the desired impression, designing and creating a corporate logo needs careful consideration. In Publisher, you can create a logo entirely from scratch or you can use the logo Wizard to make the job a little easier, or simply to gain some ideas. Most importantly, take your time. To create a logo using a Publisher Wizard, carry out the steps below:

To include a logo on every page of your document, you can place the logo in the background as described on page 30, *The page background*, Chapter 2.

You can make the presence of a logo more subtle, by converting a logo into a watermark graphic and placing it on the background. Watermarks are described on page 115, *Changing the colours in a picture*, Chapter 9.

1 Click the Design Gallery Object button on the Objects toolbar:

2 Click the Objects by Category tab.

3 In the Categories pane, click Logos.

4 Double-click the logo you want.

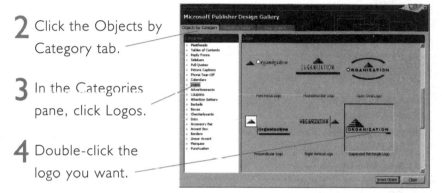

5 To replace the placeholder text with the text you want, click the text frame and type your text.

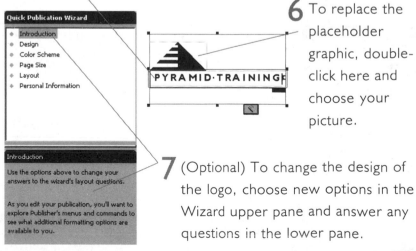

6 To replace the placeholder graphic, double-click here and choose your picture.

7 (Optional) To change the design of the logo, choose new options in the Wizard upper pane and answer any questions in the lower pane.

Creating a headline

Headlines get noticed! Just make sure that the style you choose creates the right kind of tone and level of attention. To create a headline, carry out the steps below:

1 Draw a text frame where you want the headline to appear.

2 Type the text for your headline.

3 (Optional) Make any desired formatting changes to the font, font size and style, alignment, and so on.

If a main heading is followed by further subordinate headings, create a logical structure by using a hierarchy. Format the main heading at the top of the hierarchy in larger, more bold type with a proportional space below. Then, for the remaining headings, progressively reduce the font size and proportional space as you move further down the hierarchy.

4 (Optional) Include any desired text shading.

5 (Optional) Add a text frame border if desired. You can include a plain or decorative (BorderArt) border.

6 If you include a picture or other graphic objects with your headline, group the headline text and graphic objects together.

Closed button showing grouped status. Click the button to ungroup objects

7 (Optional) Rotate the headline if desired. We rotated each chapter marker in this book 90 degrees to add contrast and to provide an easily recognizable start-of-chapter indicator.

Using a Design Gallery headline

Publisher includes several predesigned newsletter headings (mastheads) and title formats. To view these, first click the Design Gallery Object button on the Objects toolbar. With the Design Gallery dialog box displayed and the Objects by Category tab current, under Categories, click Mastheads. You can then view and choose a desired option.

Using the BorderArt Gallery

 To create ornate or unusual bullets, first, draw a box with the Rectangle tool on the Objects toolbar. Next, on the Formatting toolbar, click Line/ Border Style button followed by the More Styles command. Click the BorderArt tab and choose your desired border, followed by OK. Reduce the size of the box until it occupies a single frame of the design, and is the bullet size you require.

 Some shapes can't have BorderArt applied to them, like shapes drawn with the Oval tool or Custom Shapes tool. If the selected shape is not compatible with BorderArt, Publisher doesn't provide access to the BorderArt tab.

The BorderArt Gallery includes over 150 plain and fancy borders, which you can use to transform an otherwise dull object into something more memorable. You can add BorderArt to any rectangular shapes you create in Publisher, including picture, text, table and WordArt frames. To apply BorderArt, first click to select the object you want, then carry out the steps below:

1 Open the Format menu and click Line/ Border Style followed by More Styles.

2 Click the BorderArt tab.

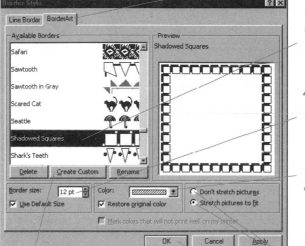

3 Click a new border.

4 (Optional) Type a new border size.

5 (Optional) Click here to change the existing colour.

6 (Optional) If you want to make your own border, click the Create Custom button.

8 Click OK.

7 (Optional) Choose whether or not pictures may be stretched.

Deleting a border

If you want to remove a border entirely, first click the object whose border you want to remove. Then click the Line/Border Style button on the Formatting toolbar, followed by the None command. Publisher then deletes the border from the selected object.

Wrapping text around a frame

Sometimes, you may want to wrap text around a picture or other graphic object. Publisher provides several options to allow you to control how and when text wraps around an object. You can:

After you wrap text around a graphic object, you can change and customize the amount of space between the object and your text. One way is to use the Picture Frame Properties command in the Format menu.

- Wrap text around a frame.

- Wrap text around the outline of a graphic object inside a frame.

- Customize the way text wraps around an object.

- Prevent text entirely from wrapping around an object.

To wrap text around the frame of an object, carry out the steps below:

1 Click the object around which you want to wrap text. To wrap text around several objects, select all the objects first.

2 If the object is layered – that is, if it is part of a stack of objects – click the Bring to Front command in the Arrange menu.

If you've chosen text wrap, but Publisher refuses to wrap text around a graphic object, the selected graphic may be set up as transparent. Try pressing CTRL+T to make the graphic opaque.

3 Now, drag the object to the desired location over the text. When you release the mouse button, Publisher re-flows the text around the frame of the object.

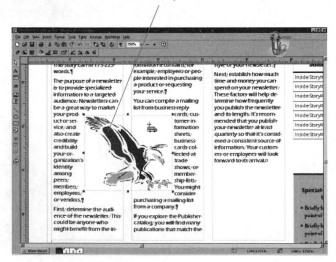

Wrapping text around a picture

If you're short of text space, wrapping text around the outline of a picture, generally creates more space for your text, and can create a more interesting balance of text and graphics.

By wrapping text around the outline of a picture or WordArt object rather than its frame, you can create some stunning design results. This approach tends to work well when the graphic object contains some element of action, tension or emotion. To wrap text around the outline of a graphic object or picture, perform the steps below:

1 Click the picture or WordArt object to select it.

2 On the Formatting toolbar, click the Wrap Text to Picture button.

If Publisher refuses to wrap text around the outline of a graphic, check if the frame is surrounded by BorderArt. Text always wraps around BorderArt. If you want text to wrap around the outline of a graphic, remove any BorderArt present.

The Wrap Text to Frame button

Text wrapped around picture outline (compare with facing page)

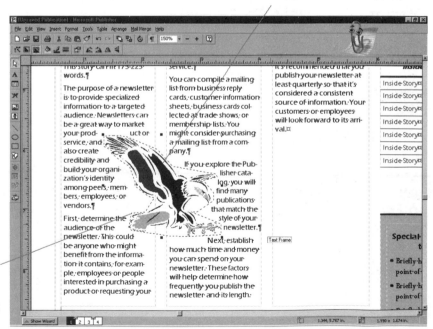

The boundary shown around a text-wrapped object does not print: it simply identifies the wrap outline.

If you change your mind, on the Upper toolbar click the Wrap Text to Frame button, to reverse the above text wrap.

Changing the text wrap shape

Notice on the previous page that although we wrapped text around the image's outline, Publisher did not wrap text entirely around it. On this occasion, this was simply because the original image of the eagle was determined by the shape you saw. However, Publisher provides the means to customize the text wrap and trace the perceived outline of the image more closely. Carry out the steps below to fine-tune a text wrap:

To prevent text from wrapping around objects, first click the text frame with the right mouse button. Next, click the Change Frame command followed by Text Frame Properties. Then, under the Options category, click the Wrap Text Around Objects box to clear the check box. Finally, click OK.

1 Click the picture or WordArt frame to select it.

2 On the Formatting toolbar, confirm the Wrap Text to Picture button is chosen.

3 Click the Edit Irregular Wrap button.

4 (Optional) If you can't see the adjust handles around the object, zoom in.

5 Place the mouse pointer over an adjust handle until you see the Adjust symbol, then drag to reshape the outline. Repeat as necessary.

When reshaping the text wrap around a picture or WordArt object, if you want to delete an adjust handle, hold down the CTRL+SHIFT keys while you click the handle you want to delete.

6 (Optional) To add more adjust handles, hold down CTRL and click on the outline where you want to place a handle.

Changing the picture/text gap

Publisher lets you change the amount of space between a picture or other object and the text which wraps around it. To change the picture/text gap, carry out the steps below:

1 With the right mouse button, click the picture or other object.

2 Click the Change Frame command followed by the Picture Frame Properties.

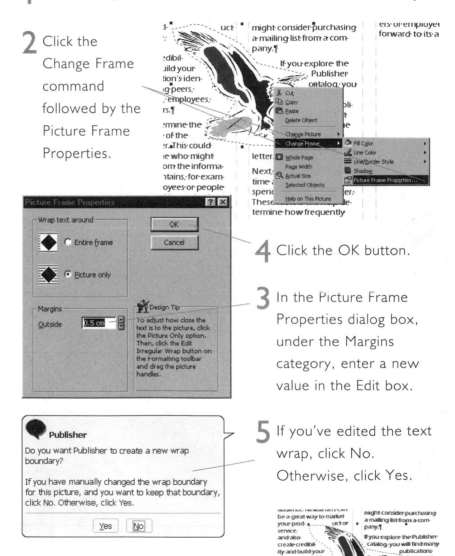

4 Click the OK button.

3 In the Picture Frame Properties dialog box, under the Margins category, enter a new value in the Edit box.

5 If you've edited the text wrap, click No. Otherwise, click Yes.

End result: in this example, we have widened the gap between the object and surrounding text

Cropping a picture in text wrap

In Chapter 9, we looked at how you can crop pictures. Remember, cropping simply means hiding part of an image. You can also crop a picture which has text wrap applied to it. To do this, carry out the steps below:

1 Click the picture you want to crop to select it.

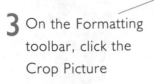

3 On the Formatting toolbar, click the Crop Picture button.

2 Make sure the Wrap Text to Frame button is active: you can't crop a picture if text is wrapped to the picture outline rather than its frame.

See Chapter 9, *Cropping a picture*, to find out more about cropping pictures.

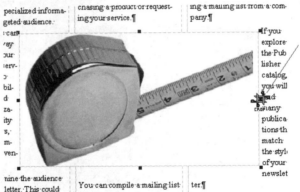

4 On the picture, place the mouse pointer over a selection handle until you see the Crop symbol.

5 Drag the selection handle to crop the picture. When you release the mouse button, Publisher wraps the text to fill in the cropped space.

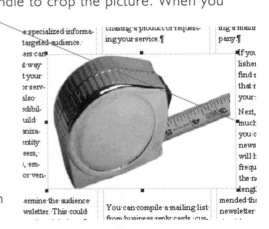

6 When finished, click the Crop Picture button again to switch off the cropping tool.

Working with pages

This chapter examines the rich variety of options open to you when working with pages in Publisher. We explore the sometimes tricky business of matching colours, how to align objects using guides, how to change page size and margins and examine what implications this has for a publication. Headers and footers and their uses are also covered. Finally, we show how to add, copy, change and delete entire pages.

Chapter Eleven

Covers

Testing different colour schemes

If you've already filled an object with a colour from the publication colour scheme, and decide to change the original colour in the colour scheme, Publisher changes the fill colours of any objects filled with the original colour to that of the new colour.

Colour schemes

A colour scheme is a special group of colours that are associated with a publication. Every Publisher document has a colour scheme, although you can define your own set if you wish. When you start a new publication, Publisher automatically applies a default colour scheme to it.

Standard colour schemes that Publisher applies to new publications are carefully chosen so that the relative colours match together. You can design your own custom colour scheme if you feel the standard colour scheme is not right for your purposes.

Changing a colour scheme

To change a colour scheme, perform the steps below:

| Click the Color Scheme command in the Format menu.

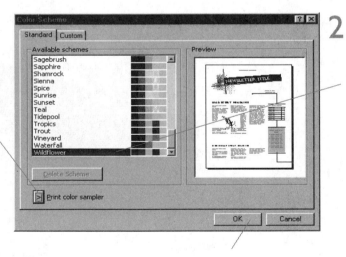

To print a sample of the selected colour scheme, with your colour printer ready to print, click here.

2 In the Color Scheme dialog box, under the Available Schemes category, click the new colour scheme you want.

A sample of the selected Colour Scheme is shown here

3 Click the OK button.

Publisher then replaces each colour from the old colour scheme applied to an object in your publication with the corresponding new colour chosen.

Creating a logo

Logos are everywhere! We see symbols of all kinds all the time. But to create the right look and put over the desired impression, designing and creating a corporate logo needs careful consideration. In Publisher, you can create a logo entirely from scratch or you can use the logo Wizard to make the job a little easier, or simply to gain some ideas. Most importantly, take your time. To create a logo using a Publisher Wizard, carry out the steps below:

To include a logo on every page of your document, you can place the logo in the background as described on page 30, *The page background*, Chapter 2.

You can make the presence of a logo more subtle, by converting a logo into a watermark graphic and placing it on the background. Watermarks are described on page 115, *Changing the colours in a picture*, Chapter 9.

1 Click the Design Gallery Object button on the Objects toolbar:

2 Click the Objects by Category tab.

3 In the Categories pane, click Logos.

4 Double-click the logo you want.

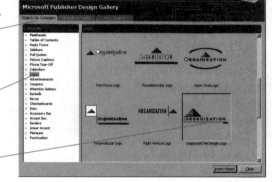

5 To replace the placeholder text with the text you want, click the text frame and type your text.

6 To replace the placeholder graphic, double-click here and choose your picture.

7 (Optional) To change the design of the logo, choose new options in the Wizard upper pane and answer any questions in the lower pane.

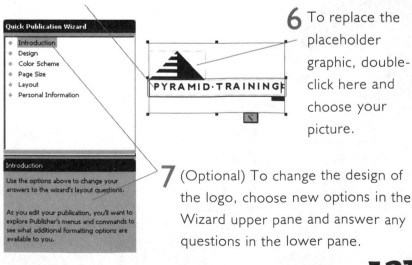

Creating a headline

Headlines get noticed! Just make sure that the style you choose creates the right kind of tone and level of attention. To create a headline, carry out the steps below:

1 Draw a text frame where you want the headline to appear.

2 Type the text for your headline.

3 (Optional) Make any desired formatting changes to the font, font size and style, alignment, and so on.

If a main heading is followed by further subordinate headings, create a logical structure by using a hierarchy. Format the main heading at the top of the hierarchy in larger, more bold type with a proportional space below. Then, for the remaining headings, progressively reduce the font size and proportional space as you move further down the hierarchy.

4 (Optional) Include any desired text shading.

5 (Optional) Add a text frame border if desired. You can include a plain or decorative (BorderArt) border.

6 If you include a picture or other graphic objects with your headline, group the headline text and graphic objects together.

Closed button showing grouped status. Click the button to ungroup objects

7 (Optional) Rotate the headline if desired. We rotated each chapter marker in this book 90 degrees to add contrast and to provide an easily recognizable start-of-chapter indicator.

Using a Design Gallery headline

Publisher includes several predesigned newsletter headings (mastheads) and title formats. To view these, first click the Design Gallery Object button on the Objects toolbar. With the Design Gallery dialog box displayed and the Objects by Category tab current, under Categories, click Mastheads. You can then view and choose a desired option.

Using the BorderArt Gallery

 To create ornate or unusual bullets, first, draw a box with the Rectangle tool on the Objects toolbar. Next, on the Formatting toolbar, click Line/ Border Style button followed by the More Styles command. Click the BorderArt tab and choose your desired border, followed by OK. Reduce the size of the box until it occupies a single frame of the design, and is the bullet size you require.

 Some shapes can't have BorderArt applied to them, like shapes drawn with the Oval tool or Custom Shapes tool. If the selected shape is not compatible with BorderArt, Publisher doesn't provide access to the BorderArt tab.

The BorderArt Gallery includes over 150 plain and fancy borders, which you can use to transform an otherwise dull object into something more memorable. You can add BorderArt to any rectangular shapes you create in Publisher, including picture, text, table and WordArt frames. To apply BorderArt, first click to select the object you want, then carry out the steps below:

1 Open the Format menu and click Line/ Border Style followed by More Styles.

2 Click the BorderArt tab.

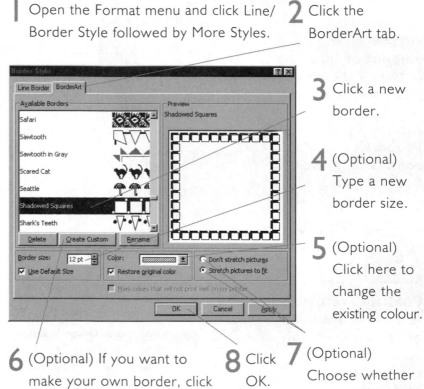

3 Click a new border.

4 (Optional) Type a new border size.

5 (Optional) Click here to change the existing colour.

6 (Optional) If you want to make your own border, click the Create Custom button.

8 Click OK.

7 (Optional) Choose whether or not pictures may be stretched.

Deleting a border

If you want to remove a border entirely, first click the object whose border you want to remove. Then click the Line/Border Style button on the Formatting toolbar, followed by the None command. Publisher then deletes the border from the selected object.

Wrapping text around a frame

Sometimes, you may want to wrap text around a picture or other graphic object. Publisher provides several options to allow you to control how and when text wraps around an object. You can:

- Wrap text around a frame.

- Wrap text around the outline of a graphic object inside a frame.

- Customize the way text wraps around an object.

- Prevent text entirely from wrapping around an object.

To wrap text around the frame of an object, carry out the steps below:

1 Click the object around which you want to wrap text. To wrap text around several objects, select all the objects first.

2 If the object is layered – that is, if it is part of a stack of objects – click the Bring to Front command in the Arrange menu.

3 Now, drag the object to the desired location over the text. When you release the mouse button, Publisher re-flows the text around the frame of the object.

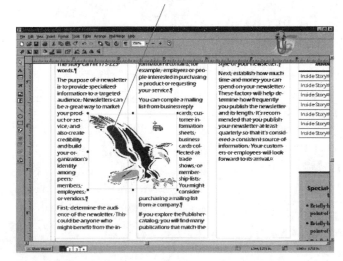

Wrapping text around a picture

If you're short of text space, wrapping text around the outline of a picture, generally creates more space for your text, and can create a more interesting balance of text and graphics.

If Publisher refuses to wrap text around the outline of a graphic, check if the frame is surrounded by BorderArt. Text always wraps around BorderArt. If you want text to wrap around the outline of a graphic, remove any BorderArt present.

The boundary shown around a text-wrapped object does not print: it simply identifies the wrap outline.

By wrapping text around the outline of a picture or WordArt object rather than its frame, you can create some stunning design results. This approach tends to work well when the graphic object contains some element of action, tension or emotion. To wrap text around the outline of a graphic object or picture, perform the steps below:

1 Click the picture or WordArt object to select it.

2 On the Formatting toolbar, click the Wrap Text to Picture button.

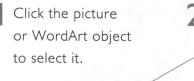

The Wrap Text to Frame button

Text wrapped around picture outline (compare with facing page)

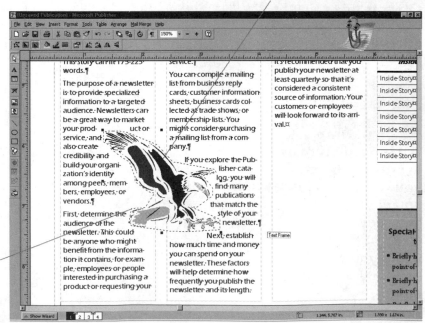

If you change your mind, on the Upper toolbar click the Wrap Text to Frame button, to reverse the above text wrap.

Changing the text wrap shape

Notice on the previous page that although we wrapped text around the image's outline, Publisher did not wrap text entirely around it. On this occasion, this was simply because the original image of the eagle was determined by the shape you saw. However, Publisher provides the means to customize the text wrap and trace the perceived outline of the image more closely. Carry out the steps below to fine-tune a text wrap:

To prevent text from wrapping around objects, first click the text frame with the right mouse button. Next, click the Change Frame command followed by Text Frame Properties. Then, under the Options category, click the Wrap Text Around Objects box to clear the check box. Finally, click OK.

1 Click the picture or WordArt frame to select it.

2 On the Formatting toolbar, confirm the Wrap Text to Picture button is chosen.

3 Click the Edit Irregular Wrap button.

4 (Optional) If you can't see the adjust handles around the object, zoom in.

5 Place the mouse pointer over an adjust handle until you see the Adjust symbol, then drag to reshape the outline. Repeat as necessary.

6 (Optional) To add more adjust handles, hold down CTRL and click on the outline where you want to place a handle.

When reshaping the text wrap around a picture or WordArt object, if you want to delete an adjust handle, hold down the CTRL+SHIFT keys while you click the handle you want to delete.

Changing the picture/text gap

Publisher lets you change the amount of space between a picture or other object and the text which wraps around it. To change the picture/text gap, carry out the steps below:

1 With the right mouse button, click the picture or other object.

2 Click the Change Frame command followed by the Picture Frame Properties.

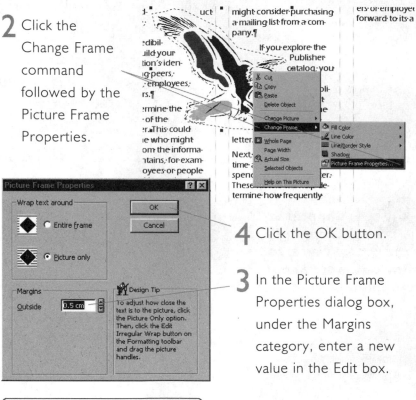

4 Click the OK button.

3 In the Picture Frame Properties dialog box, under the Margins category, enter a new value in the Edit box.

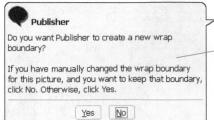

5 If you've edited the text wrap, click No. Otherwise, click Yes.

End result: in this example, we have widened the gap between the object and surrounding text

Cropping a picture in text wrap

In Chapter 9, we looked at how you can crop pictures. Remember, cropping simply means hiding part of an image. You can also crop a picture which has text wrap applied to it. To do this, carry out the steps below:

1 Click the picture you want to crop to select it.

3 On the Formatting toolbar, click the Crop Picture button.

2 Make sure the Wrap Text to Frame button is active: you can't crop a picture if text is wrapped to the picture outline rather than its frame.

See Chapter 9, *Cropping a picture,* **to find out more about cropping pictures.**

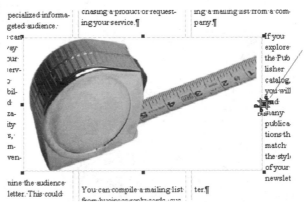

4 On the picture, place the mouse pointer over a selection handle until you see the Crop symbol.

5 Drag the selection handle to crop the picture. When you release the mouse button, Publisher wraps the text to fill in the cropped space.

6 When finished, click the Crop Picture button again to switch off the cropping tool.

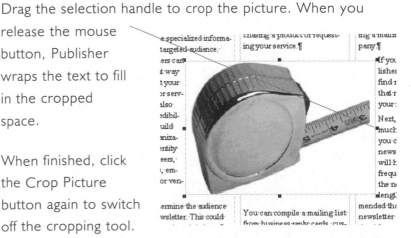

Changing a Design Gallery object

After you've placed a Design Gallery object, you can still experiment with different designs. Here's how:

| On the object, click the 'Wizard: Click to start' button.

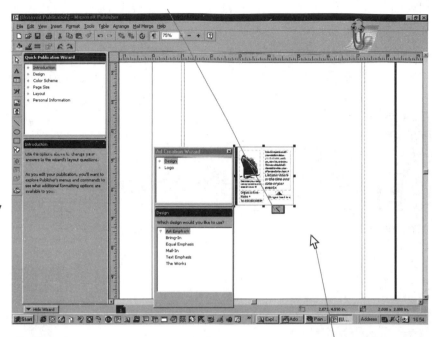

 Sometimes, only one pane is displayed. This is normal; the results depend on your choices.

2 Choose the options you want: click an option in the top pane, then answer the questions displayed in the lower pane.

3 To close the Wizard, simply click any empty space on the page or workspace.

Adding objects to the Design Gallery

With every new publication, Publisher creates an empty design set. You can add design elements to the current document design set, to the design sets that come with Publisher, or to objects from other compatible documents. On this page, we're going to add objects to the current document design set. To do this, perform the steps below:

I Click the design element you want to add to the current design set.

Objects you add to the Design Gallery are not, by default, available to any other Publisher documents. However, you can import them at any time (see the lower DON'T FORGET icon on page 126).

Text File...
Picture
Design Gallery Object...
Add Selection to Design Gallery...
Object...
Form Control
HTML Code Fragment
Personal Information
Ω Symbol...
Date and Time...
Page Numbers
Page...   Ctrl+Shift+N

2 Click the Add Selection To Design Gallery command on the Insert menu.

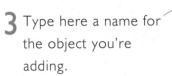

3 Type here a name for the object you're adding.

4 Click the Category you want from the drop-down list or type a new Category name here.

5 Click OK to add the object to the desired Category.

6 Save the current publication. Any objects you add to the Design Gallery for this publication are then saved as part of the publication's design set.

Deleting Design Gallery objects

You can delete objects that you store in the Design Gallery listed under the Your Objects tab, for the publication you're currently working on. However, you can't delete any of Publisher's own Design Gallery objects – that is those available from the Objects by Category and Objects by Design tabs.

To delete a Design Gallery object, perform the steps below:

After you've deleted a Design Gallery object, it's not really deleted until you save the current publication.

If you delete an object by mistake, simply close the current publication without saving it, then reopen the publication – the 'deleted' object will still be available.

1 Click the Design Gallery Object button on the Objects toolbar:

3 Under the Categories pane, click the Category containing the object you want to delete.

2 Click here to display your objects.

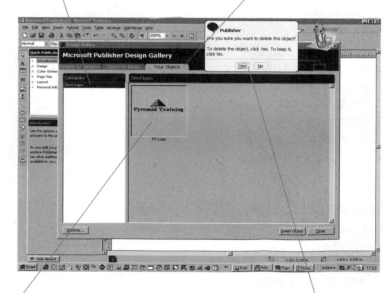

4 In the right pane, click the object you want to delete to select it.

5 Press the DELETE key.

6 Click Yes in the following prompt box to confirm you want to delete the object.

Creating Design Gallery Categories

You can create a new Category and add it to the design set of the current publication. On this page, we're going to look at how to add a new Category to the current document. Carry out the steps below to do this:

To rename a Design Gallery Category, with the Design Gallery displayed, click the Your Objects tab. Perform steps 3 and 4 below and highlight the Category you want to rename. Click the Rename button. Type a new name and click OK.

To quickly delete a Design Gallery Object Category, do this. First, click the Design Gallery Object button on the Objects toolbar. Next, click the Your Objects tab. Perform steps 3 and 4 and highlight the category you want to delete and click the Close button.

1 Click the Design Gallery Object button on the Objects toolbar:

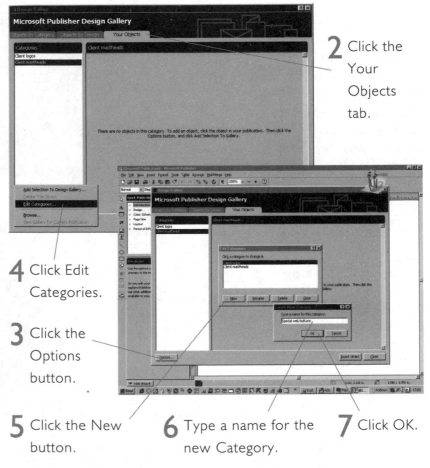

2 Click the Your Objects tab.

4 Click Edit Categories.

3 Click the Options button.

5 Click the New button.

6 Type a name for the new Category.

7 Click OK.

Publisher only records the changes you've made to the Design Gallery when you save the current publication. Therefore, it's a good idea to save immediately after making any important changes here.

Creating a custom colour scheme

You can create an entirely new colour scheme or replace perhaps only one or two colours from an existing scheme by carrying out the steps below:

1 Click the Color Scheme command in the Format menu.

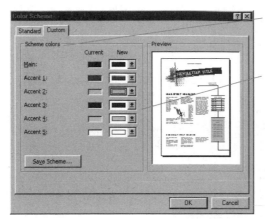

2 Click the Custom tab.

3 Under the Scheme colors category, for the first colour you want to change, click the arrow button to display the colours palette.

To fill an object with a colour from the scheme colour set, first click the object to select it. Next, on the Formatting toolbar click the Fill Color button. Then under the Scheme Colors category, click the new colour you want.

4 Click the colour effect you want. Click More Colors to see a wider range of colours. To see different effects, click the Fill Effects button.

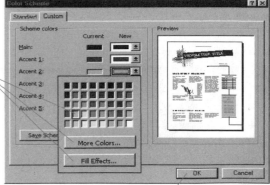

5 For every other colour you want to change, perform steps 3 and 4.

6 Click the OK button to apply your new custom colour scheme to the current publication.

Publisher then replaces each colour from the old colour scheme applied to an object in your publication with the new colour chosen.

Viewing a two-page spread

Many multi-page publications, like the newsletter shown below for instance, require printing on both sides of the paper. When you're viewing a publication on the screen with two pages side by side – just like this book – Publisher considers this form of layout as a two-page spread.

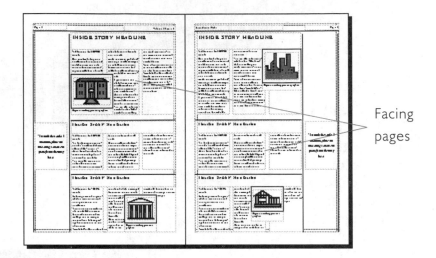

Facing pages

If a publication has three or more pages, you can opt to view facing pages side by side, as a two-page spread. To do this, open View menu and click Two-Page Spread. To switch back to single page view, open the View menu and click the command again to clear the tick mark.

Two-page spread design considerations

When establishing the structure of a document containing facing pages, it's a good idea to apply some special consideration to the design. For example, consider the following:

- Documents with facing pages generally need wider inner margins to allow for the folding or binding after the document is printed.

- Decide whether you want the left and right pages to look the same in terms of layout, or whether you want each to mirror the other (as shown above).

Changing page size

Your publication page size can be different to the paper page size. The paper page size is the size of paper you choose to print on, for example, A4. The publication page size is the size you specify for your publication. For example, you might create a size A3 publication; but this could be made up from printed A4 sheets (called tiles), which you could then photocopy or take to a printer to create the final product. To change the paper size, do the following:

Remember, if you design a publication for one printer, but later decide to set the document up for another printer, you may have to carry out a considerable amount of work correcting the page layout for the new target printer.

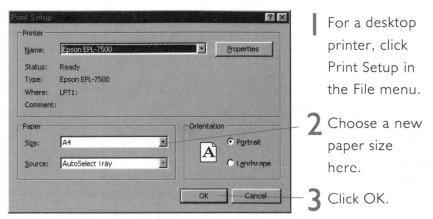

1 For a desktop printer, click Print Setup in the File menu.

2 Choose a new paper size here.

3 Click OK.

To set up a publication page size that is smaller or larger than the paper page size, click Page Setup in the File menu, then perform the following steps:

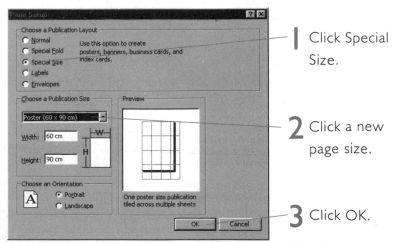

1 Click Special Size.

2 Click a new page size.

3 Click OK.

Changing page margins

Page margins are the spaces at the top, bottom, left and right edges of your pages, which are outside of the area where you place text or graphics. Publisher identifies the inner edge of page margins with non-printing dotted lines.

When you start a new document, Publisher applies a single column with 2.5cm margins around the page. However, you can change top, bottom, left and right margins. Carry out the steps below to change the size of margins:

If you change page margins after laying out a publication, you may have to realign text and graphic objects. Therefore, set margin sizes at the start of your new publication.

Open the Arrange menu and click the Layout Guides command.

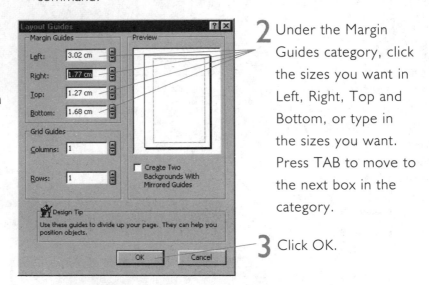

2 Under the Margin Guides category, click the sizes you want in Left, Right, Top and Bottom, or type in the sizes you want. Press TAB to move to the next box in the category.

3 Click OK.

Displaying and hiding margin guides

If you can't see a margin guide that you know should be there, it may be hidden behind opaque objects.

Alternatively, if you can't see any guides at all, the Hide Boundaries and Guides command in the View menu may be switched on.

To re-display page margins and other guides and boundaries, click Show Boundaries and Guides in the View menu.

If you set up your headers and ...ers to display ...very page, but ... pages don't ...ar to contain a ...der or footer, ...ke sure that ...'ve not placed or ...wn an opaque ...ject over the ...ader or footer ...ea.

To quickly delete a header, footer, or page number marker, first move to background view. Then, with the right mouse button, click the header, footer, or page number text frame to select it. In the floating menu, click Delete Object. Finally, click Go to Foreground in the View menu.

Adding headers and footers to facing pages

To include headers and footers in publications containing facing pages, like this book, first make sure you're viewing both pages side by side. If not, click the Two-Page Spread command in the View menu. Then click the Go to Background command also in the View menu. Carry out steps 1 and 2 on the previous page to create a header or footer. Now carry out the steps below:

1 On the Arrange menu, click the Layout Guides command.

2 In the Layout Guides dialog box, click the Create Two Backgrounds With Mirrored Guides check box, to place a tick mark in the box.

3 Click the OK button to place the mirrored headers or footers on the pages. If you want to change either the left or right header or footer, you can edit the desired header or footer now.

4 Click the Go to Foreground command in the View menu to return to the normal page display.

Hiding headers and footers on the first page

If you don't want headers and footers to appear on the first page of a publication, first move to background view and note what objects other than your headers and footers are placed on the background. Then, move to foreground view and display the first page in your document. If the header and footer are the only objects on the background, open the View menu and click the Ignore Background command.

But if you placed other objects besides headers and footers on the first page background, simply create a text frame to cover only each header or footer you want to hide. When you print, the empty text frame hides the header or footer.

Using layout and ruler guides

If the Snap To ... commands are active, when you move an object close to a layout guide, ruler guide or another object, Publisher applies a 'magnetic' pull to the object you moved, snapping it accurately into position.

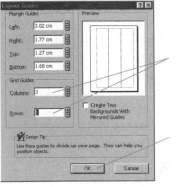

To align a ruler guide exactly with a ruler mark, make sure the Snap to Ruler Marks command in the Tools menu is switched on. If there is no tick mark next to the command, click it to turn it on. Then, drag a ruler guide to the ruler mark you want.

Publisher provides layout guides and ruler guides to help you align text and graphic objects accurately on the page. Each layout guide you insert is repeated on every page in a publication and appears as a blue or pink dotted line, whereas you add ruler guides to individual pages only when you need them. Publisher displays ruler guides as green dotted lines.

Use layout guides when you want to create a framework of rows and columns on which to plan your publication. To set layout guides in your publication, first click Layout Guides in the Arrange menu. Then carry out the steps below:

1 Enter the number of rows and columns you want here.

2 Click OK to apply your chosen layout guides.

To apply a ruler guide to your publication, first hold down the SHIFT key, then place the mouse pointer on the horizontal or vertical ruler. When the mouse pointer changes to the Adjust pointer, drag the ruler guide onto the page where you want it. To move or delete a ruler guide, hold down SHIFT and place the mouse pointer over the ruler guide you want to move or delete until you see the Adjust pointer. Then drag the guide where you want it or off the page if you want to delete it.

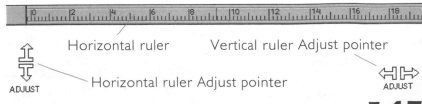

Horizontal ruler   Vertical ruler Adjust pointer

ADJUST   Horizontal ruler Adjust pointer   ADJUST

Snapping to guides and rulers

In the previous section, we looked at how ruler and layout guides can help you line up objects. However, to align objects accurately Publisher provides the Snap-to feature. The Snap to Ruler Marks, Snap to Guides, and Snap to Objects commands are included in the Tools menu. If the Snap To commands are switched on, when you move an object close to a layout guide, ruler guide, or another object, Publisher applies a kind of magnetic pull to the object you moved, 'snapping' it accurately into position.

 If the Snap to Guides command is switched on, Publisher will still snap objects to guides even if guides are hidden.

 **To snap several objects at the same time, select all the objects you want to snap, by holding down SHIFT while you click each object you want. Next, place the mouse pointer over one of the selected objects until you see the Mover symbol. Then drag the objects to the desired location and snap into position.**

Switching the Snap To commands on and off

You can turn the Snap To commands on or off simply by clicking the desired command. When a Snap To command is switched on, Publisher places a tick mark next to it. To turn a Snap To command off, simply click the desired command to hide the tick mark that was placed next to it.

The Tools menu showing the Snap to Ruler Marks and Snap to Guides commands switched on. In this example, Snap to Objects is not switched on

How Snap To affects objects already in position

Changing the status of a Snap To command does not affect objects already positioned before you chose the command. If you want those objects to snap also, simply drag them into position.

The precedence rule

If all three Snap To commands are switched on when you're aligning objects, Publisher applies the precedence rule. First, Publisher tries to snap to the nearest guide. If no guide is near, Publisher tries to snap to an object, but if no object is available, Publisher snaps to the nearest ruler mark.

Using headers and footers

...cont'd

Headers and footers contain text and about your publication, like page num section title, horizontal lines, and so o placed at the top of a page and footers Remember, you place the objects you w every page on the background. To add he to your current document, first open the click Go to Background. Then carry out th

 You can arrange for Publisher to ignore headers, footers and other background items on specific pages. This feature is particularly useful if you don't want headers and footers to appear on the first page of your publication. In foreground view, simply move to the page you want, then click the Ignore Background command in the View menu.

Draw a text frame where you want to place

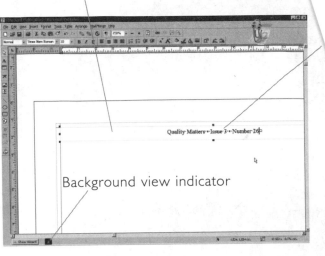

Background view indicator

 When adding page numbers, if you type a number instead of inserting the page number marker while in background view, Publisher places that same number on every page when you return to foreground view.

3 Open the View menu and click Go to Foreground to return to normal foreground view.

Inserting page numbers

To insert page numbers, create a header or footer as described above, except when you come to step 2, optionally type any text you want, like 'Page', then leave at least one space, and don't type any numbers. Next, open the Insert menu and click the Page Numbers command. Publisher inserts a hash symbol (#) as the page number marker. Finally, click Go to Foreground in the View menu. In foreground view, page number markers appear as page numbers.

Using layout and ruler guides

If the Snap To ... commands are active, when you move an object close to a layout guide, ruler guide or another object, Publisher applies a 'magnetic' pull to the object you moved, snapping it accurately into position.

To align a ruler guide exactly with a ruler mark, make sure the Snap to Ruler Marks command in the Tools menu is switched on. If there is no tick mark next to the command, click it to turn it on. Then, drag a ruler guide to the ruler mark you want.

Publisher provides layout guides and ruler guides to help you align text and graphic objects accurately on the page. Each layout guide you insert is repeated on every page in a publication and appears as a blue or pink dotted line, whereas you add ruler guides to individual pages only when you need them. Publisher displays ruler guides as green dotted lines.

Use layout guides when you want to create a framework of rows and columns on which to plan your publication. To set layout guides in your publication, first click Layout Guides in the Arrange menu. Then carry out the steps below:

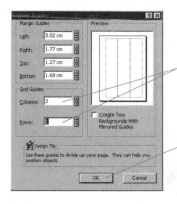

1 Enter the number of rows and columns you want here.

2 Click OK to apply your chosen layout guides.

To apply a ruler guide to your publication, first hold down the SHIFT key, then place the mouse pointer on the horizontal or vertical ruler. When the mouse pointer changes to the Adjust pointer, drag the ruler guide onto the page where you want it. To move or delete a ruler guide, hold down SHIFT and place the mouse pointer over the ruler guide you want to move or delete until you see the Adjust pointer. Then drag the guide where you want it or off the page if you want to delete it.

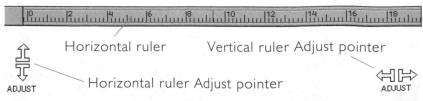

Horizontal ruler   Vertical ruler Adjust pointer

ADJUST   Horizontal ruler Adjust pointer   ADJUST

Snapping to guides and rulers

In the previous section, we looked at how ruler and layout guides can help you line up objects. However, to align objects accurately Publisher provides the Snap-to feature. The Snap to Ruler Marks, Snap to Guides, and Snap to Objects commands are included in the Tools menu. If the Snap To commands are switched on, when you move an object close to a layout guide, ruler guide, or another object, Publisher applies a kind of magnetic pull to the object you moved, 'snapping' it accurately into position.

If the Snap to Guides command is switched on, Publisher will still snap objects to guides even if guides are hidden.

Switching the Snap To commands on and off

You can turn the Snap To commands on or off simply by clicking the desired command. When a Snap To command is switched on, Publisher places a tick mark next to it. To turn a Snap To command off, simply click the desired command to hide the tick mark that was placed next to it.

To snap several objects at the same time, select all the objects you want to snap, by holding down SHIFT while you click each object you want. Next, place the mouse pointer over one of the selected objects until you see the Mover symbol. Then drag the objects to the desired location and snap into position.

The Tools menu showing the Snap to Ruler Marks and Snap to Guides commands switched on. In this example, Snap to Objects is not switched on

How Snap To affects objects already in position

Changing the status of a Snap To command does not affect objects already positioned before you chose the command. If you want those objects to snap also, simply drag them into position.

The precedence rule

If all three Snap To commands are switched on when you're aligning objects, Publisher applies the precedence rule. First, Publisher tries to snap to the nearest guide. If no guide is near, Publisher tries to snap to an object, but if no object is available, Publisher snaps to the nearest ruler mark.

Using headers and footers

You can arrange for Publisher to ignore headers, footers and other background items on specific pages. This feature is particularly useful if you don't want headers and footers to appear on the first page of your publication. In foreground view, simply move to the page you want, then click the Ignore Background command in the View menu.

When adding page numbers, if you type a number instead of inserting the page number marker while in background view, Publisher places that same number on every page when you return to foreground view.

Headers and footers contain text and graphic information about your publication, like page numbers, publication or section title, horizontal lines, and so on. Headers are placed at the top of a page and footers at the bottom. Remember, you place the objects you want to repeat on every page on the background. To add headers and footers to your current document, first open the View menu and click Go to Background. Then carry out the steps below:

1 Draw a text frame where you want to place a header or footer.

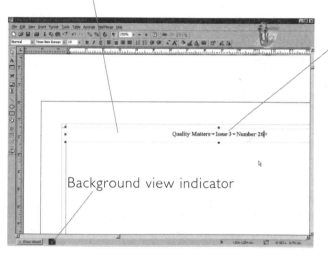

Background view indicator

2 Type and format the text you want and optionally include any graphic elements, like horizontal lines, and so on.

3 Open the View menu and click Go to Foreground to return to normal foreground view.

Inserting page numbers

To insert page numbers, create a header or footer as described above, except when you come to step 2, optionally type any text you want, like 'Page', then leave at least one space, and don't type any numbers. Next, open the Insert menu and click the Page Numbers command. Publisher inserts a hash symbol (#) as the page number marker. Finally, click Go to Foreground in the View menu. In foreground view, page number markers appear as page numbers.

Adding headers and footers to facing pages

To include headers and footers in publications containing facing pages, like this book, first make sure you're viewing both pages side by side. If not, click the Two-Page Spread command in the View menu. Then click the Go to Background command also in the View menu. Carry out steps 1 and 2 on the previous page to create a header or footer. Now carry out the steps below:

If you set up your headers and footers to display on every page, but some pages don't appear to contain a header or footer, make sure that you've not placed or drawn an opaque object over the header or footer area.

1 On the Arrange menu, click the Layout Guides command.

2 In the Layout Guides dialog box, click the Create Two Backgrounds With Mirrored Guides check box, to place a tick mark in the box.

3 Click the OK button to place the mirrored headers or footers on the pages. If you want to change either the left or right header or footer, you can edit the desired header or footer now.

4 Click the Go to Foreground command in the View menu to return to the normal page display.

To quickly delete a header, footer, or page number marker, first move to background view. Then, with the right mouse button, click the header, footer, or page number text frame to select it. In the floating menu, click Delete Object. Finally, click Go to Foreground in the View menu.

Hiding headers and footers on the first page

If you don't want headers and footers to appear on the first page of a publication, first move to background view and note what objects other than your headers and footers are placed on the background. Then, move to foreground view and display the first page in your document. If the header and footer are the only objects on the background, open the View menu and click the Ignore Background command.

But if you placed other objects besides headers and footers on the first page background, simply create a text frame to cover only each header or footer you want to hide. When you print, the empty text frame hides the header or footer.

Adding a page

You can easily add pages anywhere in your document. To add pages, first use the Page Navigation/control buttons at the lower left of the Publisher window to move to the page where you want to add extra pages.

Next, open the Insert menu and click the Page command. Then carry out the steps below:

If you're working on a two-page spread publication, it's easier to maintain the publication page pattern by adding pages in even numbers.

The Page command in the Insert menu is greyed-out (unavailable) while you're in background view.

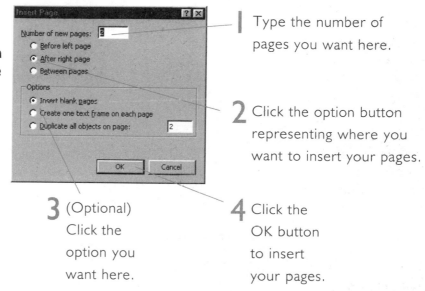

1 Type the number of pages you want here.

2 Click the option button representing where you want to insert your pages.

3 (Optional) Click the option you want here.

4 Click the OK button to insert your pages.

When you insert pages, Publisher copies any text, graphics or guides placed on the background to your new pages.

If you can't see the background layout guides

If you've inserted your new pages but can't see the layout guides you placed on the background, you may have clicked the 'Create one text frame on each page' option under the Options category in the Insert Page dialog box. This causes Publisher to place a new text frame on top of any guides.

The quickest way to remedy this situation and remove the new text frame is to click in the middle of the text frame with the right mouse button, to select the frame and display the floating menu. Then, click Delete Object. Repeat the delete action on each new page created.

Copying a page

Sometimes, pages in a document can contain common elements. In Publisher, you can copy an entire page easily, then you can make the minor changes to each page as desired. This feature is especially useful if the page you're copying from, has a particularly complex and precise structure.

To copy an entire page, first note the page number of the page you want to copy, then move to where you want to copy your page. Now carry out the steps below:

If you copy to the wrong page, immediately click the Undo button, or click Undo in the Edit menu.

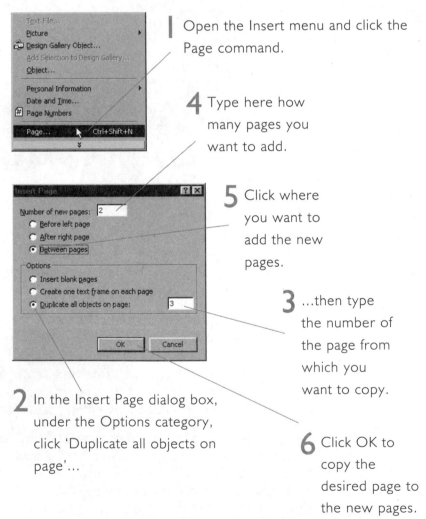

1 Open the Insert menu and click the Page command.

4 Type here how many pages you want to add.

5 Click where you want to add the new pages.

3 ...then type the number of the page from which you want to copy.

2 In the Insert Page dialog box, under the Options category, click 'Duplicate all objects on page'...

6 Click OK to copy the desired page to the new pages.

Changing the look of a page

If you want a border to appear on every page in your publication, draw the border on the background (see page 30 for more information about the page background).

If you can't see the Formatting toolbar, first click anywhere on the Standard toolbar with the right mouse button. Then click the word Formatting.

When filling a page with a pattern, to avoid losing the clarity of your message in the pattern, it's usually best to stick with larger text sizes and clear, bold fonts like Arial.

Placing a border around a page

Placing a border around a page is similar to simply drawing a box. However, while deciding the size of your border box, make sure you don't draw in your printer's unprintable region (see page 159). Perform the following steps:

1 Click the Rectangle tool on the Objects toolbar.

2 Move the mouse pointer to where you want the uppermost left corner of your border to appear.

3 Hold down the left mouse button while you drag the mouse diagonally towards the lower-most right corner of the page. Release the button when you see the desired size.

4 On the Formatting toolbar, click the Line/Border Style button.

5 On the floating menu that appears, click the More Styles command.

6 In the Border Style dialog box, choose the options you want, then click the OK button.

Filling a page with a colour or pattern

Perform the following steps, but please note the BEWARE tip in the margin to maintain adequate contrast:

1 Perform the steps above to draw a rectangular border around the page (or the area you want to fill).

2 On the Formatting toolbar, click the Fill Color button.

3 From the floating menu that appears, choose the colour and optionally the Effect you want to fill the page with.

4 On the menu bar, click Arrange to open the Arrange menu, then click the Send to Back command.

Deleting a page

If there are text or graphic objects on the page(s) you are deleting which you want to keep, drag the items you want onto the non-printing workspace area before you delete the page(s).

If you're viewing a two-page spread when you choose the Delete Page command, to maintain the structure of your document, it's usually easier to delete both pages. However, always keep a spare backup copy of your publication.

The Delete Page command in the Edit menu is greyed-out (unavailable), when you're viewing a publication in background view.

If you decide you no longer want a specific page in a publication, you can delete it easily. Once you delete a page, but change your mind and want to keep it, remember Publisher 2000 provides multiple levels of Undo (up to 20). Therefore, click the Undo button on the Standard toolbar, ideally immediately after deleting your page(s).

If a page contains text in a frame which is part of a chain of text frames on other pages, when you delete the page, Publisher re-flows the text in the linked frames to the other text frames in the chain.

So although you may have deleted the page, text that was present on the deleted page may still be present on other pages. To prevent this from happening, delete the text on the page first before you delete the page.

To delete a page, first move to the page you want to delete. Then carry out the steps below:

1 Open the Edit menu and click the Delete Page command.

2 If you're viewing a single-page spread, Publisher immediately deletes the page(s) you've chosen.

3 If you're viewing a two-page spread, Publisher displays the Delete Page dialog box. Click the option you want.

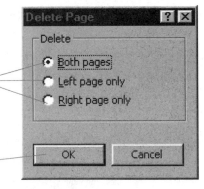

4 Click the OK button to confirm your page delete choices.

Checking and previewing your work

You're almost ready to print or publish, but before you do, in this chapter, we examine how to use Publisher's powerful document-checking tools to help ensure the text and layout of your publication are perfect.

Covers

Chapter Twelve

Checking text spacing

After you've entered text into a publication, Publisher can check your text for any extra spaces between words. Because of the neat way in which many proportionally-spaced fonts are designed, you no longer need to insert two spaces at the end of a sentence: one is adequate. Furthermore, with justified text, two spaces after a full stop can cause unsightly 'rivers of white space' appearing across your document when printed.

To search your text for double (or more) spaces after words, first click an insertion point to the left of the first character in the text frame you want to check. Next, open the Edit menu and click the Replace command. Then, carry out the steps below:

If you want to change the way Publisher automatically hyphenates words, first click in the text block you want to hyphenate. Then, open the Tools menu and click the Language command followed by the Hyphenation command. Next, choose your desired options and click the OK button. Any connected text blocks in a chain are also re-hyphenated.

1 In the 'Replace' dialog box, click here and press the SPACEBAR twice to enter two spaces.

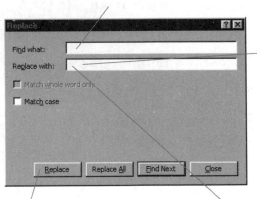

2 Press the TAB key to move the insertion point to the 'Replace with' box.

You can also use Publisher's powerful search and replace tool to quickly replace multiple occurrences of a word or phrase.

4 Click the Replace All button.

3 In the 'Replace with' box, press the SPACEBAR once.

5 Repeat the entire procedure as many times as necessary to remove all double – or more – spaces.

Repeat this procedure for all the text frames in your document you want to check. Text frames containing larger font sizes can probably be checked quicker visually.

Correcting errors while you type

Introducing AutoCorrect

While entering text, it's easy to make common errors – perhaps more so for intermittent touch-typists. For example, we may develop a habit of typing 'nad' when we really meant to type the word 'and'. Publisher, however, includes AutoCorrect – a clever facility to help automatically correct these sorts of errors.

 Whenever you're typing text in Publisher, try to get into the habit of being aware when you enter text incorrectly. Once a pattern is identified, that's the ideal time to enter it into Publisher's AutoCorrect feature while the event is fresh in your mind. Then you can forget about it knowing that AutoCorrect will identify and correct any future errors of this type.

To gain a better understanding of how AutoCorrect works, perform the following steps. First, make a list of words or phrases that you often misspell, making sure that you write each word or phrase exactly as you often misspell it. Using the example above you would write 'nad' for 'and.' Then carry out the steps below:

1 Open the Tools menu and click the AutoCorrect command.

2 Make sure the 'Replace text as you type' check box includes a tick mark. If it doesn't, click it.

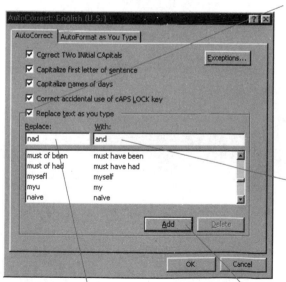

4 In the 'With' box, enter the correct spelling of the word or phrase entered in the 'Replace' box.

3 In the 'Replace' box, type the first word or phrase on your list that you often misspell.

5 Click the Add button.

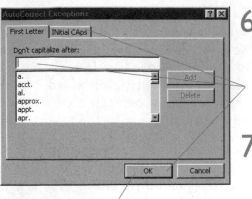

6 If there are any special exceptions to the rule, click the Exceptions button and make your choices then click OK.

7 Perform steps 3 to 6 for all the other words on your list.

8 Click the OK button to confirm your choices.

 To replace computer-standard quotes or hyphens with the more professional typesetter's equivalents, do the following. First, click AutoCorrect in the Tools menu. Then in the AutoCorrect dialog box, click the AutoFormat as You Type tab. Make sure the 'Replace: "Straight quotes" with "Smart Quotes" check box contains a tick mark, then click OK.

Preventing AutoCorrect misspelling special words or acronyms

Some words can be spelt in several ways. The word 'reference' for example is often abbreviated to 'ref.', and normally AutoCorrect would ensure a capital letter occurs after a full stop is entered. If you want to use a particular spelling, you can ensure AutoCorrect does what you want in these special occurrences. Perform the steps below:

1 Open the Tools menu and click AutoCorrect.

2 Click the Exceptions button.

3 Click the First Letter tab.

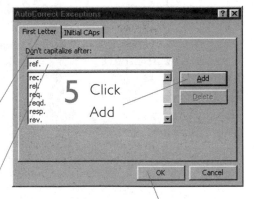

4 In the 'Don't capitalize after' box, type the exact word – including full stop – after which you don't want Publisher to capitalise.

6 Click the OK buttons to close dialog boxes.

Checking spelling

To check spelling in a text or table frame, first click the text or table frame you want, to select it. Next, open the Tools menu and click Spelling, followed by the Check Spelling command. Then carry out the steps below:

The Check Spelling command in the Tools menu is greyed-out (unavailable) if you click a WordArt frame. Check the contents of WordArt frames visually.

1 Publisher will only display the Check Spelling dialog box if it finds a word that it does not recognise. If the dialog box does not appear, Publisher could find no misspellings and the spell check is complete.

2 Publisher places each word it does not recognise in the 'Not in dictionary' box. Perform either step 3, 4 or 5 below.

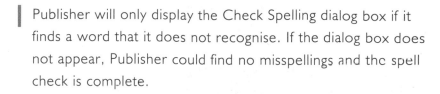

3 Click Ignore to ignore this instance of the word.

7 Click Close to hide the dialog box.

4 Or click Change, to change the word to the word in the 'Change to' box; or, if other words are available, click another word in the Suggestions box.

6 (Optional) To tell Publisher to check all text and table frames in a publication, click 'Check all stories'.

5 Or click Add to add the word to the dictionary. Publisher then ignores the word.

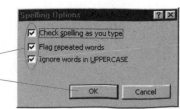

Note: you can also change the spelling options. See margin

To change the way in which Publisher checks spelling, open the Tools menu and choose Spelling, followed by Spelling Options. Then make your changes in the dialog box and click OK to finish.

Using the Design Checker

Publisher provides the Design Checker for checking the layout of a publication, and tries to identify problems that may prevent the publication from printing normally.

For example, in the dialog box opposite, Publisher has identified an object placed on the non-printing area of the page.

You can check specific pages or an entire publication. To start the Design Checker, open the Tools menu and click Design Checker, then carry out the steps below:

1 By default, Publisher automatically opts to check the layout of an entire publication; if you want to do this, simply click OK.

3 Or, if you want to check specific pages, click Pages.

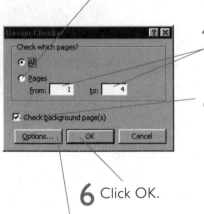

4 Next, type the page range in the From and To boxes.

5 Make sure a tick mark is present here if you want Publisher to check the design layout on the page background also.

6 Click OK.

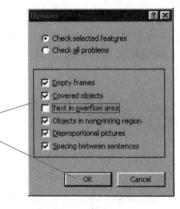

2 Or you can tell Publisher to check only for specific problems. Click the Options button, then in the Options dialog box, click the options you want, followed by OK.

7 If Publisher detects a layout problem, it displays an appropriate dialog box.

8 You can then move back to your publication and fix the problem.

 The Design Checker dialog box stays on the screen until you click Close. If this, or any other dialog box, is blocking a clear view of your publication, click the mouse pointer on the dialog box Title bar and drag the box away.

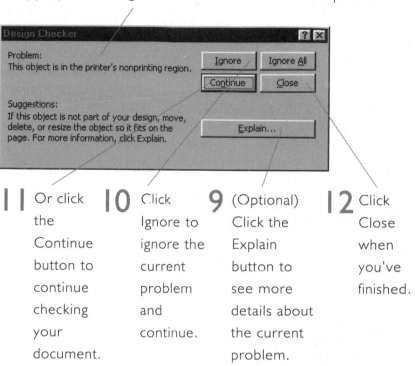

11 Or click the Continue button to continue checking your document.

10 Click Ignore to ignore the current problem and continue.

9 (Optional) Click the Explain button to see more details about the current problem.

12 Click Close when you've finished.

 If your printer's Properties settings doesn't contain a Paper tab, examine your printer's documentation for information about its unprintable area.

After a document has been checked once, Publisher may display a dialog box asking if you want to run the Design Checker again to make sure no further layout errors exist. Click Yes to start the Design Checker or No to end the session.

A word about your printer's unprintable region

Most printers aren't able to print exactly to the edge of the paper. This unprintable area varies from printer to printer. Usually, you can determine your printer's unprintable region by first clicking the Start button, followed by Settings, then Printers. Click on your printer's icon using the right mouse button and choose Properties. Click the Paper tab (or similar) and look for information you want.

Previewing your publication

When you reach this stage, you've come a long way. Congratulations! Let's review what you've done already. You have:

- Assembled a publication successfully.

- Run a spell-check.

- Checked for irregular text spacing.

- Used Publisher's excellent Design Checker.

- Corrected any minor irregularities that may have arisen due to carrying out these latest checks.

Now you can view your masterpiece on the screen as it will look when printed. Perform the following steps to view your publication with boundaries, guides, and special characters hidden:

 In the View menu, if you don't see the Hide Special Characters command and the Hide Boundaries and Guides commands, they are already turned on.

 To re-display hidden boundaries, guides and special characters, in the View menu, click Show Boundaries and Guides and Show Special Characters.

To see a full-page view of your publication, open the View menu and click the Zoom command followed by the Full Page command.

2 Open the View menu again and click the Hide Special Characters command.

3 Open the View menu and click Hide Boundaries and Guides.

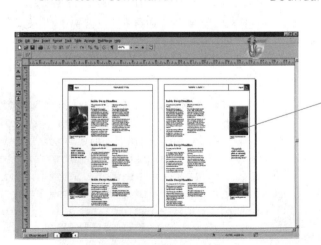

An example screen shot with boundaries, guides and special characters hidden

Printing and e-mailing a publication

If you're not interested in publishing to the Web, printing a paper-based publication is the crowning glory of all your efforts. In this chapter, we explain how to print a publication and examine some of the options open to you when you print. We also take a closer look at the implications of using an outside printing organisation, including special precautions you can take to help ensure your publication is output exactly as you intended. Finally, we explain how to send a publication by e-mail.

Covers

Chapter Thirteen

Printing the date and time

If you're intending to print several drafts of a publication, it's useful to know when you printed each draft. Publisher provides a command which inserts the date or time in the publication.

To insert the date or time, click in the text frame where you want it to appear or draw a new text frame. Next, open the Insert menu and click the 'Date and Time' command. Then carry out the steps below:

1 Under the 'Available formats' category, click the date or time format you want.

By using the Print Date or Time option, you can keep a permanent log of all your printouts. This can be useful when verifying dates and times with printers and work colleagues.

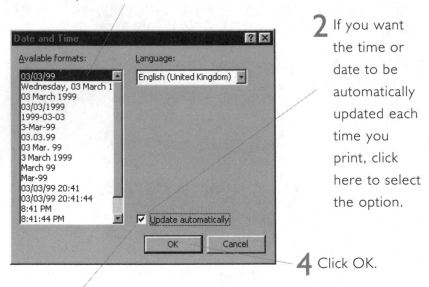

2 If you want the time or date to be automatically updated each time you print, click here to select the option.

4 Click OK.

3 Alternatively, if you want to insert the time or date as it is now, click here to delete the tick mark. However, remember, if you clear this option, Publisher will no longer automatically update the date or time.

Note: although we have illustrated the above example using a text frame, you can also include this option in a table frame. In this context, Publisher considers a table to simply be a more formalised text frame.

Printing on special paper

Providing you've not chosen to use an outside printer (see the DON'T FORGET icon in the margin) you can still create an attractive, professional, coloured finish to your publications, without incurring the higher costs often associated with using several colours. You could try using pre-printed coloured paper stock.

 If you've chosen to print to an 'outside' commercial printer (see pages 19–21 for details of how to set this up), the Special Paper command in the View menu may not be available (shown greyed-out on the menu).

PaperDirect is a company that produces a range of coloured papers and patterns. Publisher includes 42 coloured styles which you can use. You choose a style, add the text and graphics you want, then simply print. However, remember that before printing you need to load your printer with the appropriate paper.

To use the special paper options, first open the View menu and click Special Paper. Then perform the steps below:

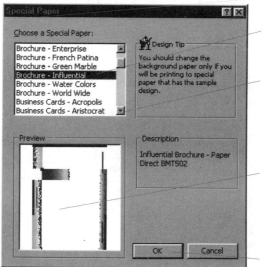

 Printing using the special paper option is an excellent way to create a consistent and stylish corporate identity including business cards, complement slips, letterheads, and so on, at a modest price.

1 Click the pattern style you want.

2 (Optional) Click the scroll buttons to see more patterns.

3 See the preview image of your chosen pattern.

4 Click OK.

Now you can add the text and graphics you want, then print as explained overleaf when ready.

To stop using special paper patterns and clear the screen, first open the View menu and click Special Paper. Then, under the 'Choose a Special Paper' category, click None, followed by OK.

Printing to a desktop printer

When you started your publication, you established which printer you want to use to print your publication. To print a publication *whose size is smaller* than the paper you're printing to, first make sure your printer is online and ready to print. Next, open the File menu and click Print. Then carry out the steps below:

You can change or specify further choices for your printer, including paper size, graphics and colour options (if applicable) by clicking the Properties button and making your choices in the dialog boxes.

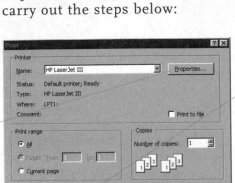

| If the Page Options button is visible, click it and go to step 2; otherwise, go to step 6.

2 To print several publication pages on each sheet of paper, follow steps 3 and 4. To print a single copy per sheet, go to step 5.

To print on non-standard-sized paper, first open the File menu and click Print Setup. Then, under the Paper category, click the paper size you want. Next, in the Source box, click Manual feed (if available), followed by OK.

5 Click the 'Print one copy per sheet' option button, followed by the OK button.

4 To change the distance between the pages on each sheet of paper, click the Custom Options button, make your changes and click OK. Then go to step 6.

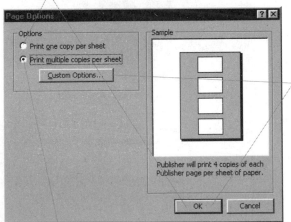

3 Click 'Print multiple copies per sheet'.

To quickly print an entire publication without displaying the Print dialog box and without changing any default print options, click the Print button on the Standard toolbar:

7 Click here to choose which pages you want to print.

6 (Optional) If you want to change this value, click here to establish the number of copies you want printed.

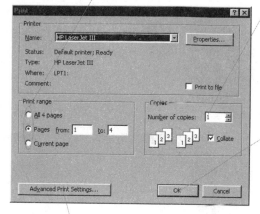

12 Click OK.

In the Print dialog box, when there is only one page in a publication, Publisher makes the Pages option unavailable (greyed-out).

8 (Optional) Click here to display the Advanced Settings dialog box.

9 (Optional) Choose the Options you want here.

10 (Optional) Crop marks help you trim a publication when it is smaller or larger than the paper size to which you're printing. Click here to include crop marks on your printouts.

When you print, Windows creates temporary files on your hard disk. Therefore, it's a good idea to make sure that you have at least 10 Megabytes of hard disk space free to ensure problem-free printing.

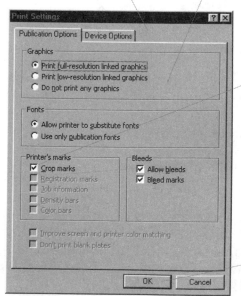

11 Click OK to clear the dialog box.

To print a publication *whose size is larger* than the paper you're printing to, first make sure your printer is online and ready to print. Next, open the File menu and click Print. Then carry out the steps below:

2 Choose the options you want here.

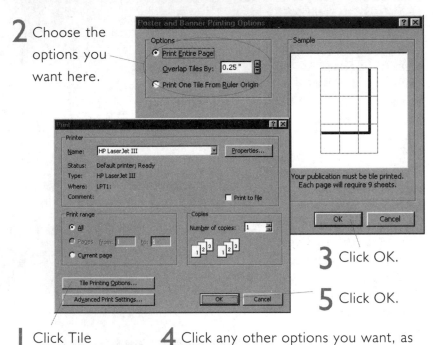

3 Click OK.

5 Click OK.

| Click Tile Printing Options.

4 Click any other options you want, as described on the previous page.

Using the Print Troubleshooter

If your publication doesn't print the way you expect it to, or won't even print, you can use Publisher's Print Troubleshooter. By default, Publisher loads the Print Troubleshooter when you print. You can also access the Print Troubleshooter at any time, simply by clicking Print Troubleshooter command in the Help menu.

However, you can turn off the automatic status of the Print troubleshooter. Here's how: Choose the Options command in the Tools menu, followed by the Print tab. Then click the 'Automatically display Print Troubleshooter' check box and click OK.

Using an outside print shop

 If you're delivering your publication to your chosen print shop on disk, you can copy the Publisher files using the Pack and Go command on the File menu.

To produce a large quantity of copies of your publication, or to produce a better quality finish than you can achieve from your desktop printer, consider using an outside print shop. You can print a master copy to hand to your printer or you can deliver your completed publication on disk in Publisher format, or as a file, or you can send your publication to a print shop using a modem. However, speak to your print shop representatives first to find out exactly what they require from you.

Printing quality and resolution issues

If you're using a commercial printer, you can use:

 If your publication is too large to fit onto a single floppy disk, you can use a file compression program. Talk to your print shop representatives about this.

- Spot colour: suitable when all colours and shades in a publication are made up from one or two 'real' colours. This option provides high-quality output which can be relatively inexpensive.

- Full-colour separations: ideal if your publication contains colour photographs or more than two shades of colour other than black and white. But remember, this option can be particularly expensive.

- Black and white with shades of grey: here printing quality can be excellent and cost can be quite reasonable. But it may be worthwhile shopping around, as prices may vary considerably.

Printing to a file

 If you decide to print your publication to a file, discuss this option in detail with your printing service first. You can discover more information by typing: 'Create an EPS file' into the Publisher Help system.

If your print shop wants you to deliver your publication as a file, here's what you do. After saving your file in Publisher, open the File menu and click Print. In the Print dialog box, click the 'Print to file' check box to place a tick mark in it. Make sure that all of your desired printing options and properties have been chosen. Then, click OK. In the Print To File dialog box, type a name for your file. Then change to the folder in which you want to store the PostScript file and double-click the folder you want. Finally, click OK. Publisher saves your publication as a file, with the filename extension of .prn. You can then copy this file to a disk or send it via modem to your chosen printer.

Establishing trapping values

Over-printing prints black or dark coloured text and objects on top of any lighter coloured background colour. By default, Publisher overprints imported pictures, lines, fills and dark coloured text.

In commercial colour printing, while a publication is being printed, the paper or printing plates can shift or stretch slightly and misregistration of the inks can occur. However, Publisher allows you to compensate for these effects by using two key techniques: trapping and overprinting (see hints in margin for more information).

Publisher can apply trapping only when you print colour separations and separations are used only when you choose process- or spot-colour printing (see pages 20–21 for more information). When you start a new publication, by default, Publisher does not apply any trapping. If you decide to use trapping, you can use the default setting suggested by Publisher or you can apply your own. Publisher follows its own set of sophisticated rules to determine trapping values. To apply automatic trapping, perform the steps below:

Where two different coloured objects meet, trapping works by extending the lighter colour so that it overlaps slightly into the darker coloured object. This ensures that no gaps appear where there should be none and so avoids any misregistration.

1 Open the Tools menu and choose the Commercial Printing Tools command.

2 Then choose the Trapping command followed by the Preferences command.

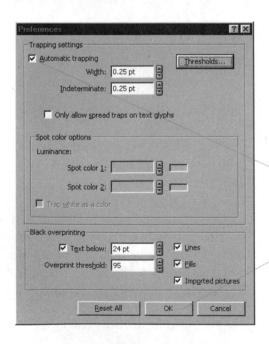

3 Click the 'Automatic trapping' check box to add a tick mark.

Before applying any trapping, speak to your print shop: they may prefer to set the values.

4 Click the OK button to confirm your changes.

Embedding fonts in a publication

If you're planning to print your publication on another computer, the other computer may not have the fonts you have used in your publication installed. However, by embedding the fonts you use in your publication, you can ensure that you can print or view your publication correctly on another computer.

 When you use the Pack and Go command, by default, Publisher turns on font embedding. However, you can choose not to embed fonts when running the Pack and Go Wizard: simply uncheck the Embed TrueType Fonts check box.

Publisher can embed TrueType fonts in the current publication when the fonts are not already installed in Windows and providing the fonts you use allow embedding. However, Publisher embeds *only* TrueType fonts and all the fonts included with Publisher automatically have full embedding rights.

To embed fonts in a publication, perform these steps:

1 Open the Tools menu and choose 'Commercial Printing Tools'.

2 Then choose the Fonts command.

3 If you want to embed TrueType fonts when you save a publication, click here to place a tick in the box.

For lots more information about embedding fonts, see the Publisher online Help under the topic: 'About Publisher Font Embedding for Commercial Printing'.

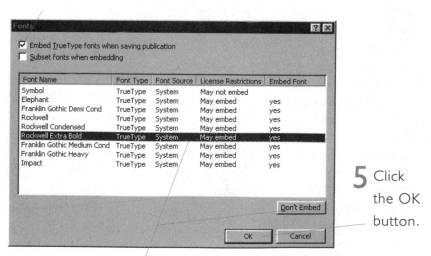

5 Click the OK button.

4 To change the embed status of a specific font, click the font you want, then click the Don't Embed button.

Sending your publication by e-mail

E-mail is an ideal medium to use if you want to pass on or obtain important information relatively quickly. Depending on how your Windows installation was set up – i.e, if you chose to install the Microsoft Mail (or compatible) options during Setup/upgrade of Windows – Publisher may provide the Send command on the File menu to enable you to send a Publisher document to a compatible recipient using e-mail. Otherwise, this command is hidden.

As the e-mail procedure can be intricate, it's a good idea to make sure that you're familiar with your e-mail program, before attempting to use the Send command.

To send a Publisher file as an attachment to an e-mail, first make sure that you've saved your publication. Click the Send command in the File menu. You may need to click OK in the following dialog box to display your default e-mail reader's 'send' dialog box. Then perform the following steps:

| Enter the e-mail address here of the person to whom you're sending the document.

You can reduce the amount of time needed to e-mail a publication by using a file compression program like WinZip to compress a publication before e-mailing. WinZip is shareware and is available from most shareware vending Web sites, or on CD-ROMs that often accompany PC magazines.

3 Click Send.

2 Include a brief description of what you're sending here.

Your publication is then sent as an attachment to your e-mail message. You can learn more about sending files as attachments from your Microsoft Windows and your e-mail applications' Help documentation.

Creating a compelling Web site

In this final chapter we introduce and define the Internet and World Wide Web, and explain how you can create, modify, check and preview your Web site using Publisher's powerful yet easy-to-use Web site creation tools. Then, when you're ready, we explain how to publish your Web site to the Web and create a truly global impact. Have fun, and good luck!

Covers

Chapter Fourteen

Introducing the World Wide Web

At the time of writing, using the Internet, you can send and receive information anywhere across the globe using one of the many free ISPs that are emerging, for only the cost of local phone calls.

Compared to a paper-based advertising budget, your Web budget can be small by comparison, yet may be just as effective – or even more so – while being less wasteful in resources.

The Web is growing quickly. Globally, over 200 million subscribers are now online – 1 billion are expected by 2005! (source: Motorola 1999 survey).

The Internet and the World Wide Web (WWW): words we often hear used interchangeably, but which in fact are not the same thing. While the Internet is a network that allows data to be carried between computers across the globe, the WWW simply provides an easy way of viewing and navigating the data that is stored on the tens of thousands of computers that make up the Internet.

Today, anyone – companies, organisations and individuals – with access to a PC, modem and hence to the Internet, can advertise or market themselves and their products on the Web. Companies, small and large, can advertise to up to 55 million people worldwide – and this number is rising daily – for mere pence per day. Research carried out by the International Data Corporation – at http://www.idcresearch.com – suggested that by the close of year 2000, 163 million users will have access to the Web! Arguably, this has already been achieved (see margin).

The Web provides a new avenue to enable any organisation to attract customers worldwide, 24 hours a day, at low cost. Individuals can also set up their own 'Home Page', simply as a means to contact other individuals who share the same interests, or to advertise their skills, their wares, and to display their CVs to potential employers.

The Internet and the Web, even now are rich in new possibilities and nobody *really* knows where the Web is going. But Microsoft have ensured, with Publisher 2000, that their publishing product will not be left behind. Publisher's Web tools are refreshingly easy to use and simple to apply, yet are powerful and flexible. The remainder of this chapter explains how you can produce your own Web pages in Publisher quickly and effectively.

The benefits of having a Web site

On your Home or Index page, tell your visitors to bookmark the page immediately, so they can always find your site again easily.

The Internet is a great leveller: both small and large firms can market themselves on a level playing field.

For many businesses, information is the new currency, and the Web is now one of the most powerful tools to gain access to the most up-to-date information quickly.

For businesses, organisations and clubs

A carefully designed compelling Web site can provide a powerful way in which to keep in contact with a wide range of potential customers, existing customers or members. Once your clients have recorded or 'bookmarked' your Web site, you can easily keep in contact with them using Web promotions, features, special offers and so on. Here are some of the more important benefits:

- Contact thousands of prospects cheaply using only your well designed Web site and the awesome power of e-mail (or if you get it right, maybe millions – so if you're serious, start making contingency plans!).

- Easy access to a vast and wide range of information: there's something for everyone on the Internet!

- An international, global audience: you're no longer constrained by national boundaries.

- The Internet is an ideal low cost way to test new products or ideas.

- Some products may only be profitable for the small business when sold on the Internet!

- Most Internet users have disposable income (computer, modem, software, credit card, etc.): this means you can have access to a defined affluent customer base who have the capacity to spend money – if won over.

For individuals

You can establish a Web page simply because you want to prove you can do it and the fact that you have that option. This is as good a reason as any other. Some individuals, however, may want to enhance their careers, impress their boss or even provide an all-singing, all-dancing CV-oriented Web site, ready for those all-important job interviews. The main theme to remember if you want to build up *and* maintain the number of visitors: provide something unique, valuable or attractive on your Web site.

Avoiding Web page design pitfalls

Creating a Web site is no longer a difficult undertaking. A wide variety of software tools are available to help you, including: *FrontPage* from Microsoft and shareware offerings like Luckman's *WebEdit Pro*. But it's easy to get carried away by adding components that may do little to add to the value and useability of a Web site.

If you publish material on the Web that you don't own, ensure that you have copyright or permission to do so, to avoid possible costly litigation.

Design for success

For businesses however, effective Web site design is crucial. **For a business-oriented Web site, every single component that goes to make up the site must contribute in some way to sales.** This last sentence cannot be overstated: it is so important. Ruthlessly cut out every excess word, component or anything that does not really contribute to your Web site's theme. And particularly avoid using larger graphics that take a long time to download! Through applying a little thought and consideration, you can create an effective, compelling Web site that captures your prospects' attention and compels them to buy.

Don't apply watermarks to Web pages. Why? The watermarked graphic in the background will almost certainly slow down the download speed of your Web page – many visitors won't wait too long.

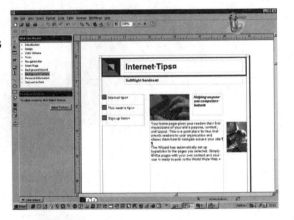

Learn about how to avoid Web page design pitfalls in *Web Page Design*, also in the 'in easy steps' series.

Aim to have your Web site listed in the top 20% of sites found by the major search engines – it can be done! Research on the Net how others – often one-person organisations – are doing just that right now.

The great thing about the Internet is how individuals and small organisations can project an image as good as – and sometimes better than – those of the larger organisations investing hundreds of thousands of pounds a year into their Web site programs.

The Web Site Wizards

Using Publisher's Web Site Page-Wizard, you don't need to know anything about the HTML Web page language. Publisher treats Web pages in the same way as other forms of documents.

To display the Catalog dialog box, simply open the File menu and click the New command.

After completing your Web site design, if you have a Web browser installed (like Microsoft Internet Explorer), you can preview and check your Web site before publishing to the Web. (Internet Explorer 5 is included in all editions of Office 2000.)

The quickest way to create a Web site in Publisher is to use the Web Site Wizards and let Publisher do most of the design work for you. When you start the Web Site PageWizard, Publisher asks you some basic questions about what kind of Web site you want to create, and prompts you for details you want entered.

After the Wizard has done its work, you can still modify the design as described later in this chapter. To start the Web Site PageWizard, open the File menu and click the New command, then carry out steps 1 to 4 below:

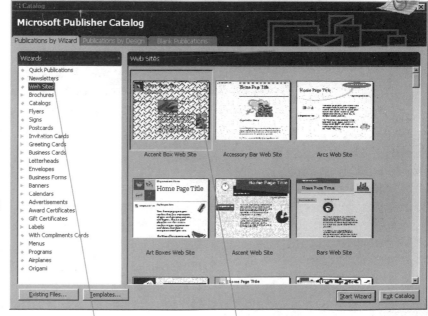

1 Click Web Sites.

2 Double-click the design you want.

3 Answer the Wizard's questions and make your choices.

You can quickly create interesting single- or multi-page designs tailored for business, community or personal use. Also, Publisher's Web graphics are designed for downloading quickly: **an important feature**.

To quickly replace a graphic placeholder with another image, double-click the image you want to replace to display the Insert Clip Art dialog box.

 To replace a graphic placeholder with a picture stored on your hard disk, but not from the Clip Gallery, click the picture you want to change. Then, open the Insert menu and click the Picture command followed by the From File command to display the Insert Picture File dialog box.

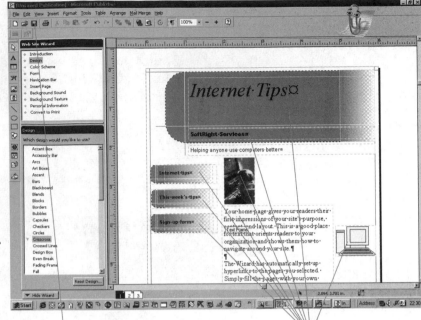

 To download clip art and photos from the Microsoft Clip Gallery Live Web site, click the Clips Online button in the Insert Clip Art dialog box.

5 Click here to save your Web site publication.

4 After the Wizard has created your Web page(s), click/double-click (see the HOT TIPs) on each text and graphic placeholder and replace with your own text or graphic.

To assist you in choosing graphics to include on your Web pages, Microsoft has developed hundreds of pictures in the Clip Gallery which are especially 'tuned' for use in Web pages. Some are animated to provide an added element of interest to your Web pages. Sound clips too are available and can provide the finishing touch to help create a really stunning presentation.

Also, by clicking the Design Gallery Object button on the Objects toolbar, you can see a range of e-mail buttons, Navigation bars and page dividers which you can include on your Web pages. You can view these objects organised in categories or as design set elements. To learn more about the Design Gallery, see Chapter 10.

Creating Web pages your way

A hyperlink is like a key providing access to another part of the Web. When you click on a hyperlink, you immediately move to where the link is pointing.

Instead of using the Hyperlink command in the Insert menu, you can click the Hyperlink button on the Standard toolbar:

If you've upgraded from Publisher v2.0, v95, v97 or v98, you can create a Web page based on an existing template. Click New in the File menu. Then, click the Templates button and choose the template you want.

Even though Publisher provides a wide range of pre-designed Web page templates, you may prefer to create your own masterpiece from scratch. If you're creating an entirely new Web page, simply add the desired text, graphics, tables, WordArt or any other objects just as you would with any other Publisher document. However, if you're adding Web-related items like hyperlinks (see margin), Web page backgrounds and textures, a different approach is needed.

You can create a hyperlink (see margin for explanation) to another part of the same document, another Web document, or another part of the Web. And your hyperlink can be highlighted text, a selected object, or part of a selected object.

To create a hyperlink from an object, first select the object you want to change to a hyperlink. Next, click the Hyperlink command in the Insert menu. Then carry out the following steps:

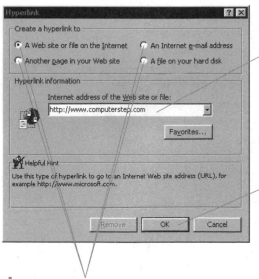

2 Under Hyperlink Information, enter the address to which you want the hyperlink to point.

3 Click the OK button. When you complete this operation for a text hyperlink, Publisher changes the colour of the text to indicate its new status.

| Under the 'Create a hyperlink to' category, click the type of hyperlink you want.

To create a hyperlink from a part of a selected object, first click the Hot Spot Tool button on the Objects toolbar. Then drag the crosshair mouse pointer over the object to trace the rectangular shape and position you want. Finally, in the Hyperlink dialog box, choose your desired link option as described on the previous page.

Including a textured or coloured background

Complementary colours and textures can create depth and stimulate added interest in your Web site. Publisher provides a range of textures and colours which you can apply to your Web pages. To add a background colour or texture to your Web page, first click the 'Color and Background Scheme' command in the Format menu. Then carry out the steps below:

1 To add a background texture perform steps 2–5. To add a solid background colour, perform step 6.

2 Click the Texture box to place a tick mark in it.

3 Click Browse then double-click the texture you want in the Web Backgrounds dialog.

 With this dialog box, you can also change the Colour Scheme or create customised colours for the background.

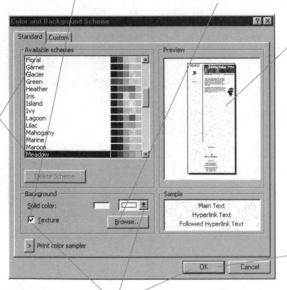

4 (Optional) A sample of your texture is shown here. If you change your mind, perform step 2 again and make a new choice.

5 Click OK.

 The Color and Background Scheme command in the Format menu is only available when you're working with Web pages.

6 To change the background to a solid colour, first click the Texture box to clear it. Click the down-arrow next to 'Solid color'. You can then choose a colour from the Color Palette. To see a wider range of colours, click More Colors. To see shading and tints, click Fill Effects. Click OK to finish.

Including animated graphics

Publisher converts any rotated text, BorderArt, and gradient text fills used in text frames to graphics, which will not load as quickly as 'pure' text.

To view other Categories, use the Forward and Back buttons.

In Microsoft Internet Explorer, you can right click over an animated picture to display a menu, then chose the Save (Picture) As command to save it as a file. (Many animations are copyrighted so check first if you have legal permission to do this.)

Animated graphics – also known as animated GIFs – used in Web pages are typically smaller icon-type images that contain some moving components. An animated graphic can enhance interest in a Web page and provide an effective eye-catching focus. To include an animated picture in your Web page, insert the Publisher CD-ROM in your drive, then perform the following steps:

1 Open the Insert menu and choose Picture followed by the Clip Art command.

2 Click the Motion Clips tab.

3 Click the Category you want.

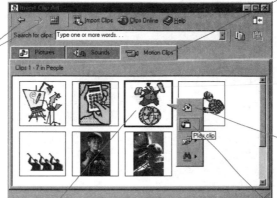

6 To place a clip on the page, click the Insert Clip button.

4 Click the animation picture you want.

5 To view an animation, click the Play Clip button.

Once the animation is placed on the page, you can resize or move it just like any other object. You can view any animated pictures you place on a Web using the Web Page Preview command which starts your default Web page browser – such as Microsoft Internet Explorer.

If you want to place an animation from a file outside of Publisher, use the Picture > From File command on the Insert menu. Alternatively, if you can view the desired animated picture in Microsoft Internet Explorer (IE), adjust the Publisher and IE windows so that you can view both windows. Then simply drag the animated picture onto the publisher window and place at the desired location.

Adding sound and video content

Once you've placed your chosen sound component on the page, you can't hear it in Publisher: instead, listen to it in your browser when you start the page (providing your PC hardware supports sound).

You can include sound as a background component so that when visitors view your page, the desired sound clip plays automatically. Sound components can be made up of music, speech, other miscellaneous sounds or a combination of any of these. To include a background sound component, perform the steps below:

1 Move to where you want to add a background sound.

2 Open the File menu and click Web Properties.

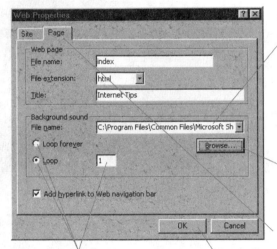

4 Enter the path name leading to the sound file you want here. Then go to step 6.

5 Click Browse and find the sound file you want, then click it.

Web browsers display plain text more quickly than pictures. If you expect most of your users may not have fast PCs, consider limiting the size, number and type of pictures or animations you use.

6 Click 'Loop forever' if you want the sound to play continuously, or click Loop and enter the number of times you want the sound to play.

3 Click the Page tab. Then perform either step 4 or step 5.

7 Click OK.

If pictures are too large and complex, they will take too long to download; users may then give up trying to view your site.

Including sound and video clips in a Web page

To place a sound or video clip anywhere on a Web page, use the Clip Gallery Tool to draw a frame. Then, from the Insert Clip Art dialog box, click either the Sounds or Motion Clips tab and click a Category. Click a desired file, followed by the Insert Clip command to place the clip on the page. A visitor, viewing the finished page in a Web browser, can click on and open the clip to listen to (or view) it.

Creating an online form

A Web page form is the electronic equivalent of a paper-based form. But a Web form can be much more valuable. Web forms are an ideal addition to a Web site if you want to gain important information and make the job of submitting this information easy for your visitors. In fact, a key point about designing a Web form is that it should be quick and easy for your visitors to complete – if it's not, unless you offer some compelling reason to stick with it, the chances are, your visitors won't bother to complete it.

When using text labels for the components of your form, keep to simple, easy-to-understand words to make the job of filling in a form online quick and easy.

What makes up a Web form

Publisher provides the following seven types of component that can be used to make up a form:

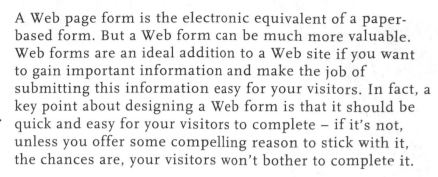

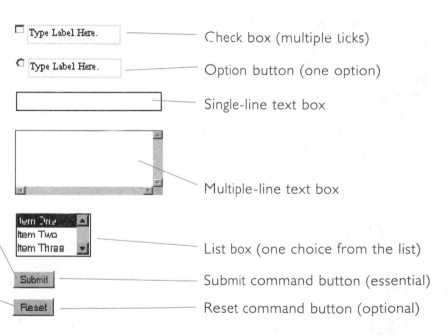

Check box (multiple licks)

Option button (one option)

Single-line text box

Multiple-line text box

List box (one choice from the list)

Submit command button (essential)

Reset command button (optional)

Every Web form must contain a Submit button. The commands associated with this button establish where to send the data gathered by the form.

A Reset button allows a visitor to clear a form and start entering data again.

Creating a form: your two choices

You can use one of the predesigned forms in the Design Gallery. Publisher provides three basic designs: an Order form, a Response form and a Sign-up form. You might need to modify the chosen form to meet with your precise requirements, although this is easy to do. Alternatively, you can design and create a form entirely from scratch.

You can create a form from scratch using the Form Control button on the Objects toolbar: Click this button to display a floating menu containing access to the seven components listed. Click your desired component, then click on the page where you want to place the component. Finally, edit to fine-tune the placement and labelling of each component used.

When you position a form object on the page, make sure the form doesn't touch other objects on the page. If other objects overlap onto the form, the form controls may not function properly. Ideally allow a clear area of free space around a Web form.

Using Publisher's predesigned Web forms

Here's one way to add one of Publisher's predesigned forms to a Web page. Perform the following steps:

1 Click the Design Gallery Object button:

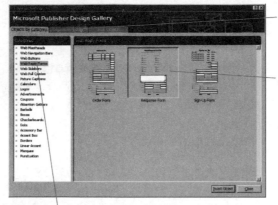

2 Click the Objects by Category tab.

4 Double-click the form you want.

5 Carefully drag the form object into position.

3 Click Web Reply Forms.

6 (Optional) Edit any desired specific parts of the form, like component label titles, currencies, and so on. Click the desired component to select it, then simply type your new entry.

The most important part: dealing with your data

Now you can decide how you want to collect the data your Web form collects. You can see the options available by double-clicking the Submit button: Publisher then displays the Command Button Properties dialog box. Three options are then available:

- Save the form data in a file stored on the Web server.

- Have the form data sent to you by e-mail.

- Collect the form data using a program from your Internet Service Provider (ISP) (Establish the Form 'Method' with your ISP or Web site host.)

Discuss your best option with your Internet Service Provider as processing forms data can be tricky to set up.

Changing your Web site's design

Text hyperlinks are easily spotted. Publisher displays each hyperlink in a different colour to the rest of your text, or the hyperlink is shown underlined.

It's a good idea to keep a backup copy of your Web site files, before changing the originals. You could use the ßackup option while saving your Web site files in the Save As dialog box.

Here's a quick way to check if an object or a piece of text is a hyperlink and if so, where it points to. Simply place the mouse pointer on top of the text or object you want to check. Publisher then displays a ScreenTip.

Creating Web pages is an evolving process. Rarely will you design a page first time without having any desire to experiment with, or change completely, its look: the business of design involves emotions, 'feel' and creativity, which can vary often. Sometimes you may also want to change the address to which a hyperlink points. Remember, you can do this for a text hyperlink or an object hyperlink; both procedures are similar to creating a hyperlink as described on previous pages.

Changing the address of a text hyperlink

To change the address to which a text hyperlink points, first select the hyperlink you want to change. Next, click the Hyperlink command in the Insert menu. Then carry out the steps below:

1 Choose one of four ways to change the location to where a hyperlink points.

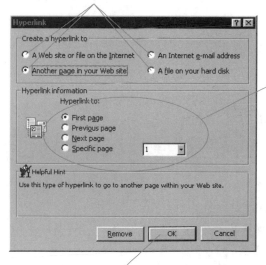

2 Here, enter the new address or page to which you want the hyperlink to point. The options available here depend on the choice you made in step 1.

3 Click OK to confirm your desired changes.

Removing (deleting) a hyperlink

Display the dialog box above as described, then click the Remove button.

To open an existing Publisher Web document, simply open the File menu and click the Open command. Publisher considers a Web document to be the same as any other publication.

The Color and Background Scheme command in the Format menu is available only when working with Web pages.

If the background colour/texture is too strong, reading Web text may be difficult for your readers, and can detract from the main points of your message. Create adequate contrast between text and background.

Changing the address of an object hyperlink

To change the address to which an object hyperlink points, first you need to establish whether the hyperlink covers an entire object or only a part of it. If the hyperlink covers an entire object, simply click the object to select it. Alternatively, if the hyperlink covers only part of an object, click on an edge of the desired hot spot on the object. Remember, a multiple hot spot object contains several hot spots, each of which could point to a different address. Then, click the Hyperlink command in the Insert menu, and carry out the steps below:

1 In the Hyperlink dialog box (shown on pages 177 and 183), under 'Hyperlink information' enter the new address or page to which you want the hyperlink to point. The precise format of this dialog box depends on the option you chose in the 'Create a hyperlink to' category. Possible options are: another document on the Internet; an Internet e-mail address; another page in your Web project; or simply a file stored on your PC's hard disk.

2 Click OK to make your changes.

Changing the background colour or texture

To change the background colour or texture, carry out the same procedure outlined previously for including a textured or coloured background, as described on page 178.

Changing non Web-specific elements of your pages

So far, we've discussed adding and changing only those elements which are in some way related to the Web. All other non Web-specific items in your Web pages like pictures, tables, WordArt, text, shapes, etc., are treated by Publisher in the same way as any paper-based document, and so will not be repeated here. See Publisher's excellent online Help for more information about designing, creating, editing and publishing a Web site.

Previewing your Web site

Before publishing your Web site to the WWW, it's a good idea to confirm your designs and highlight any problem areas using the Design Checker, as described in Chapter 12.

Use the spell checker and other proofreading tools and tips outlined in Chapter 12 to check your Web site for these types of errors.

The Web Site Trouble-shooter can help identify problems during preview. To turn it on or off, use the Options command in the Tools menu. Click the User Assistance tab and choose the option you want.

Once you have created your masterpiece, run the Design Checker and carried out spell-checking and proofreading tasks, you can preview your Web site using a Web browser installed on your PC. This will show how your Web site will appear when you publish it to the Web, and will also allow you to test the hyperlinks and to check that each hyperlink points to the address you want.

If you don't have a browser, Microsoft Internet Explorer comes on the Publisher CD-ROM. To install this browser, simply follow the instructions given in Publisher's online Help Index: *Install Microsoft Internet Explorer 5.0*, on the Publisher CD. Alternatively, contact your Internet Service Provider or vendors of other compatible Web browsers.

The following procedure for previewing a Web site assumes that you have Microsoft Internet Explorer installed:

1 Click the Web Site Preview command in the File menu, or, the Web Site Preview button on the Standard toolbar:

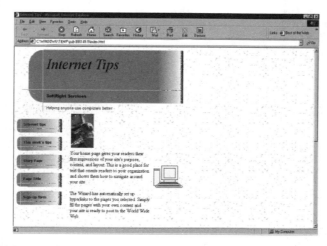

3 When all is correct, you're now ready to publish your Web site to the Web as described overleaf.

2 In your browser window, click each hyperlink: check they all work correctly. If any hyperlinks are wrong, make your changes back in Publisher while previewing and repeat steps 1–2 to check your results.

Publishing your Web site

Sometimes, an Internet Service Provider may ask you to change the filename and filename extension of your Home page. Use the options available from the Page tab of the Web Properties command in the File menu to do this.

If you can't upload your Web files using the Web Publishing Wizard, publish your Web site to a folder on your hard disk and manually upload the files: speak to your Internet Service Provider for guidelines.

To convert your Web site to HTML, use the Save As Web Page command on the File menu.

Making your Web site easy to find

Before publishing your site to the Web, you can help make your Web site more accessible via the Internet search engines. Click the Web Properties command in the File menu and enter appropriate keywords and descriptions of your Web site. Then click OK to finish.

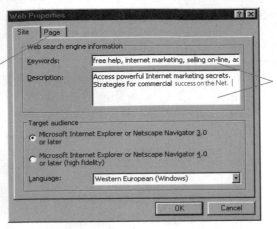

Web publishing options

Publisher provides three options:

- Publish directly to the Web. You must already have Internet access and Web space ready (see below).

- Or you can upload your Web pages later. Publish your Web site to a folder on your hard disk, for transfer to the Web later.

- Or you can publish to a network hard drive and make your Web site available on an organisation's Intranet. Click the Web Folders button in the Save As Web Page dialog box (see File menu for the command).

Using the Web Publishing Wizard

On a stand-alone PC, arguably the easiest way to publish your Web site to the Web is to use the Microsoft Web Publishing Wizard. However, to do this, you'll need to find out some key information from your Internet Service Provider or Web site host. If you don't have the Wizard installed, you can install it from the Publisher CD-ROM. For full details, see the excellent Publisher online Help section: *Publish a Web site* and *Publish using the Microsoft Web Publishing Wizard*. Good luck with your Web site and publishing with Publisher.

Index

PUBLISHER 2000

in easy steps

Brian Austin

COMPUTER
STEP

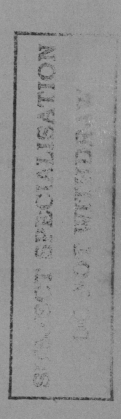

In easy steps is an imprint of Computer Step
Southfield Road . Southam
Warwickshire CV33 OFB . England

Tel: 01926 817999 Fax: 01926 817005
http://www.computerstep.com

Notice of Liability
Every effort has been made to ensure that this book contains accurate
and current information. However, Computer Step and the author shall
not be liable for any loss or damage suffered by readers as a result of
any information contained herein.

Trademarks
Microsoft® and Windows® are registered trademarks of Microsoft
Corporation. All other trademarks are acknowledged as belonging to
their respective companies.

Printed and bound in the United Kingdom

ISBN 1-84078-061-4